# COLORADO
# SCENIC GUIDE
## NORTHERN REGION

# COLORADO
# SCENIC GUIDE
# NORTHERN REGION

## Lee Gregory

Johnson Books: Boulder

Second Edition
1   2   3   4   5   6   7   8   9

ISBN 1-55566-062-2
LCCCN 90-61369

Printed in the United States of America by
Johnson Publishing Company
1880 South 57th Court
Boulder, Colorado 80301

# ACKNOWLEDGEMENTS

A project of this size requires help from many people. I would like to thank all who have assisted in this undertaking, even if I was not fortunate enough to know all of their names so that they could be listed here.

Special thanks go to Steve Reames, who has explored much of Colorado, making him well suited to offer advice. In addition to encouragement, editorial suggestions, photographs, accuracy checks, and general proofreading, Steve provided me with four-wheel-drive access to some of the hard-to-reach locations. Gratitude is also owed to Ken Jessen, author of *Railroads of Northern Colorado*, who taught me about publishing from the writer's viewpoint, and to the owner of the Calhan Paint Mines and his family for allowing me to include this site in the book.

Many friends have spent long hours reading through my manuscript to correct spelling and grammatical errors. For this effort, I thank Jean and Bob Bump, Mary Lee and Walter Gregory, Joy and Randy Hudson, Sonje and Ken Jessen, Kathy and Bill Kwinn, Katie and Charlie Potter, Steve Reames, Ron Riedel, and Jeanette and Jim Vyduna.

Many government agencies and private individuals have provided information and photographs. Gratitude is owed to the helpful employees of the National Park Service, the National Forest Service, the Bureau of Land Management, the United States Geological Survey, and the state of Colorado. In particular, I would like to thank Andrew J. Kordziel, Angelina Valverde, Andy Senti, and Evaline Olson (BLM); the staff of Pike, San Isabel, Roosevelt, Arapaho, and White River national forests; Bob Miller, Sandy Schmidt, Barbara L. Fager, Lynn E. Young, Ed Nesselroad, and André J. Coisman (USFS); Dwight F. Canfield, Carol Edwards, and Hal Chantker (USGS); Harris R. Feathers (USDA); Linda West, Glen Kaye, and Michael L. Baugher (NPS); Captain Philip J. Crowley (USAF); Jean Rubin (Colorado Division of Parks and Outdoor Recreation); Cheryl Brchan (Colorado Geological Survey); Louis Campbell (State Cartographer); Gregg Chancellor and Hal Haney (Colorado Office of Tourism); Dale B. Dixon (Two Mile High Club of Cripple Creek); Ann Bishop (Buena Vista Chamber of Commerce); Mary B. Cassidy (Leadville Chamber of Commerce); Terry Lee (Pikes Peak Country); Lucy Blake (Carbondale Chamber of Commerce); the Georgetown Chamber of Commerce; Kristin L. Murphy (Central City Chamber of Commerce); the Loveland Chamber of Commerce; Gary Miller and Keith R. Nunn (Kremmling); Ruth V. Stimack (Royal Gorge Company); Ronald R. Goss (Greater Canon City Chamber of Commerce); and Grant Carey (Cave of the Winds). Special thanks go to Dave Cooper of the Craig District BLM office, who provided me with detailed information and maps of sites in his area, and to NPS Ranger Walter Saenger who helped me with photos and information on Florissant Fossil Beds National Monument.

For help with the second edition, thanks go to Wayne Brown (Mayor of Marble), Desi Ortiz (USAF Academy), and the many others who contributed.

I would also like to thank Lynn Schmidt, John Scruggs, and Bill Parzybok for providing encouragement; Annie Epperson, who helped me for hours on end at Art Hardware; the people at Colorado Color, who worked hard at converting my color slides to black and white prints; and Barbara Mussil, Rebecca Herr, and all of the other people at Johnson Publishing Company who helped put this book together.

Timberline, Rocky Mountain National Park.

This work is dedicated to my parents for instilling in me an insatiable wanderlust and to the late Edward Abbey for being the defender and philosopher of the West.

# TABLE OF CONTENTS

# TABLE OF CONTENTS

# SCENERY COVERED BY THIS GUIDE

Colorado has something for everyone. If you're interested in scenery, archaeology, mining history, paleontology, hiking, old railroads, backpacking, Indian history, mountain climbing, or explorers, this is the place to visit.

In fact, Colorado is so diversified that a guidebook such as this is difficult to produce; the research and exploration are fun but it's painful having to decide what to leave out. In the six years of research that have gone into this book, I have read volumes of background material, studied layers of maps, evaluated piles of photographs, and visited over one thousand scenic locations. From this, I have selected one hundred sites that I think best represent the quality and diversity of Colorado's scenery. Fifty of these are included in this guide. The remaining 50 sites are found in a companion volume: *Colorado Scenic Guide: Southern Region*.

The sites included here are representative of the best scenery northern Colorado has to offer. Apart from locations of exceptional historical and scenic value, few man-made sites are included. All of the national parks and monuments within the northern region of the state are included, as are a few major natural wonders that have been commercialized.

I hope this book can convey at least a small portion of the enjoyment and fascination I have experienced while hiking, driving, four-wheeling, and flying through Colorado. I consider it a privilege to share this wonderful place with you. I hope you'll find this guide entertaining as well as useful. Enjoy Colorado's magnificent scenery!

# COLORADO BACKGROUND

Colorado, the Centennial State, was admitted to the Union on August 1, 1876. Rectangular in shape, the state extends 387 miles east-west and 276 miles north-south. The resulting area of 104,247 square miles makes it the eighth largest of the 50 states. The neighboring states are Nebraska, Kansas, Oklahoma, New Mexico, Utah, Wyoming, and an infinitesimal touch with Arizona at Four Corners, the only place in America where four states converge at a single point. The 1980 Census places Colorado's population at 2,889,000, less than 28 people per square mile. Most of the state's inhabitants reside in a north-south corridor where the mountains meet the eastern plains. There are over 9,000 miles of Colorado-maintained state and federal highways; with county and city roads, the total exceeds 82,558 miles.

Although Colorado is not the largest state, it is certainly the highest, with an average elevation of 6,800 feet. Three-quarters of all United States land above 10,000 feet is within Colorado. Only 13 peaks in the country are taller than Mount Elbert, tallest in the state at 14,431 feet. There are 53 Colorado peaks over 14,000 feet and more than 880 mountains attain a height of at least 11,000 feet. Of the peaks that line the Continental Divide, the highest are within the boundaries of the state. The lowest point in Colorado is 3,350 feet, where the Arkansas River crosses the Kansas line near Holly.

Geologically, the state can be partitioned into three major zones: the eastern high plains, the central mountains, and the western plateau. The plains constitute 40 percent of the state and are generally flat with an elevation ranging from 4,000 to 6,000 feet. The mountain regions contain foothills from 7,000 to 9,000 feet and higher peaks from 10,000 to 14,000 feet. The far western regions of the state are part of the Colorado Plateau, which extends into parts of Wyoming, Utah, Arizona, and New Mexico. This zone consists of sedimentary, desert-like plateaus from 5,000 to over 10,000 feet in elevation.

Human habitation in Colorado has been traced back more than 11,000 years to the Clovis culture. The agrarian civilization of the Anasazi in southwestern Colorado culminated in large masonry pueblos, which were abandoned about A.D. 1300. Nomadic tribes then dominated the state until the 1860s. Spanish explorers began to arrive in the early 1500s, and all of Colorado was under their claim until 1800, when France acquired the Louisiana Territory. France sold these holdings, including Colorado east of the Continental Divide, to the United States in the Louisiana Purchase of 1803. While Spain was encouraging the settlement of southern Colorado to strengthen the border of New Spain, a period of American exploration was beginning with the Pike and Long expeditions. Fur trade was established as the state's first industry by the mountain men who trekked to the Rockies to trap beaver. The Mexican War began in 1846 and ended with the Treaty of Guadalupe Hidalgo in 1848, which ceded all of the Southwest to the United States. Colorado, entirely an American territory, was soon the site of the gold rush of 1859, which propelled it into statehood.

# COLORADO BACKGROUND

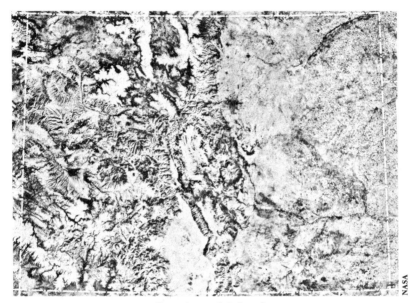

NASA

Satellite photo of Colorado.

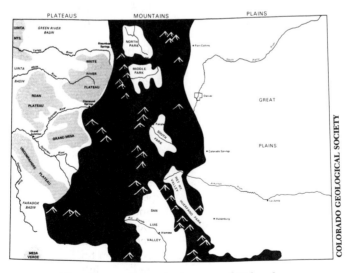

COLORADO GEOLOGICAL SOCIETY

The three major geologic zones of Colorado.

# COLORADO WEATHER

The three major geologic regions of the state—plains, mountains, and plateaus—provide a convenient means of dividing Colorado's weather patterns. One cannot always accurately describe Colorado weather in generalities, however. On the same day, one location in the state may exhibit weather conditions typical of the tropics while another, a hundred miles away, may suffer weather normal to the Arctic Circle. These variations occur not only from place to place but also at the same location between day and night. The thin, dry atmosphere of Colorado's higher elevations allows the sun's rays to penetrate easily, producing warm daytime temperatures. The same process works in reverse on clear nights by letting heat escape into space by reradiation, which causes cool nights. Thus, temperature variations of 30°F or more are not uncommon from day to night at the same location.

Despite this wide diversity, certain trends have been observed over the years. Weather on the high plains varies little from place to place even though 40 percent of the state is included within this climatic zone. Typical yearly averages for the plains are a temperature of 51°F, 14.5 inches of precipitation, and 33 inches of snowfall. Summer days are hot, with highs above 95°F not uncommon. The hottest temperatures in Colorado occur when a warm, dry air mass from the southwest moves over the eastern plains and is further heated by the sun. Winter days are usually moderate with occasional extreme nighttime lows of between 0 and -15°F. Cold air masses can move from the north to settle over the plains, causing temperatures to drop abruptly.

The plains receive little precipitation. A wet Pacific air mass must give up most of its moisture to rise over the mountains, leaving little for the eastern region of the state. A northern air mass, though cold, rarely carries much moisture. In fact, most of the rainfall on the plains is due to warm, moist air masses from the Gulf of Mexico that work their way into Colorado during the spring. As this type of air mass rises toward the Rockies, it is cooled and its moisture condenses out as rain. This condition is often referred to as up-slope, and it usually causes many overcast days in May. Even though Colorado is known for its low humidity, afternoon thundershowers, sometimes with hail, and virgas (streaks of precipitation that evaporate before reaching the ground) are quite common during the summer. Three-quarters of the plains' precipitation occurs during the growing season from April through September.

An interesting phenomenon known as a chinook wind can affect the part of the plains nearest the mountains. When the air mass is backed against the western slope of the mountains, a great deal of energy is required to push it over the peaks toward the plains. As the air spills over the top and descends to the lower elevations, it is heated by compression at an average rate of 5.3°F per thousand feet of elevation lost. With an elevation difference of up to 9,000 feet between mountains and plains, a considerable temperature increase is possible. The result is a high-speed, warm wind along the Front

# COLORADO WEATHER

Range during winter and spring. Speeds of over 130 MPH have been clocked in the Boulder area. High winds combined with snow in the plains can produce blizzards that kill livestock and strangle transportation for days. Tornadoes also occur in the plains but with less frequency, property damage, and loss of life than in states to the east.

In the mountains, weather conditions may vary greatly from place to place because of differences in altitude or other local effects. Typical yearly averages for towns in the mountains are a temperature of 40°F, 16.5 inches of precipitation, and 102.5 inches of snowfall. The great variations concealed by these averages are illustrated by Wolf Creek Pass, which has an average February temperature of 10°F and an average July temperature of 74°F with annual precipitation averaging 41 inches of moisture and 364 inches of snowfall.

Summer days in the mountain regions are usually quite pleasant, with average highs in the 60s and 70s. The nights are cool, even in July. In general, 3.2 degrees in temperature are lost for each thousand feet of elevation gained, so a hot, short-sleeve day at the bottom might be a cool, jacket day at the top. Temperatures on mountain summits may easily fall below freezing at night, even in midsummer. The mountains are often spared the grip of cold winter air masses that may inundate the plains but are too thin to reach the higher elevations. Cold air will sometimes lie in the valleys, causing low temperature extremes as severe as those on the peaks during winter. The record low for Colorado occurred in Taylor Park, a basin near Gunnison, on February 1, 1951: -60°F.

Most of the precipitation in the mountains comes from Pacific air masses. As the air rises to cross the peaks, condensed moisture falls as precipitation. In contrast to plains rainfall, most mountain precipitation occurs during the winter, with June being one of the driest months. The first snowfall usually comes in September, but accumulation doesn't begin until middle or late October. In general, the amount of local precipitation increases with altitude. Fierce winds can cause winter storms to be severe in the high country. Snowmelt in the spring causes peak stream and river runoff during late June and early July. Heavy rainfall at that time can lead to flooding and occasionally flash flooding.

The western plateau regions of Colorado have weather similar to the desert zones of Utah. In fact, daytime temperatures in the middle of summer can be unpleasantly hot. Typical yearly averages for this area are a temperature of 48°F, 13 inches of precipitation, and 53 inches of snowfall. The plateau areas have fewer dramatic changes in their weather than the other regions of the state. In comparison to the climate of the plains, the summer days are similar; the winter temperatures are just a degree or two cooler; and the spring and early summer months are much drier. The plateau region, like the mountain province, obtains its moisture from Pacific air masses.

# PRECAUTIONS

Although visiting and enjoying Colorado scenery is not generally hazardous, the following list of suggestions may be useful in planning for maximum comfort, safety, and convenience. This section identifies potential hazards so they won't come as a complete surprise and points out that there are dangers to the environment as well. Common sense is almost always the best course. There are several excellent books available that cover wilderness safety and etiquette in greater detail than is offered here.

In your vehicle you should carry:

- Food and water

- Warm clothing

- Sleeping bags or blankets (during winter)

- Chains (useful in both mud and snow)

- Tools and spare parts

- A reliable spare tire

- A flashlight

- A first-aid kit

- A compass

While hiking:

- Be prepared for any kind of weather.

- Retreat if storms approach.

- Take cover in a bad hail storm.

- Be careful where you place hands and feet while in areas that may contain rattlesnakes (plateaus, plains, and valleys below 8,000 feet).

- Check for ticks (sometimes abundant in moist, vegetated areas) during the wet part of spring (usually May and early June).

- Stay on established trails.

# PRECAUTIONS

- Don't throw rocks over the edge.

- For longer hikes, carry a flashlight, food, and water.

- Don't drink untreated water.

- Climb to higher ground if rising water indicates the danger of a flash flood.

- Return to lower elevations if symptoms of altitude sickness appear (nausea or shortness of breath).

- Wear sunglasses and protective skin creams to guard against the sun's ultraviolet rays. (This is especially important if you are around snow on sunny days.)

- Leave animals alone.

- Retreat if road conditions are too rough or hazardous for your vehicle.

- Plan to return from the backcountry before dark.

- Never trespass.

- If you are exposed to a lightning hazard (indicated by the crackle of static electricity, ionizing or glowing air, or your hair standing on end), retreat to the lowest area that you can reach quickly and crouch into a low position with your feet held tightly together as your only contact with the ground.

- Be aware that distances given on signs are not always accurate.

- Stay on established roads.

- Lock your car.

- Be careful with fire while camping.

- Pack out your trash when you leave the backcountry.

# KEY TO INFORMATION BLOCK

**TYPE:** This entry identifies the scenic nature of the site.

**ADMINISTRATION:** This entry identifies ownership of the site. Land administration is subject to change. Even if this guidebook indicates the site was once on public land, please do not trespass if that land is now marked as private. In the case of private property, please view the site from public land or a public road. Never enter private land without the specific permission of the landowner. National parks, monuments, recreation areas, forests, and grasslands as well as Bureau of Land Management areas and sites administered by state, county, and local governments are open to the public, though a visitation fee may apply.

**QUALITY:** The relative scenic quality of each site is described by the following terms in order of least scenic to most scenic: SCENIC, VERY SCENIC, EXTREMELY SCENIC, SUPERBLY SCENIC.

**ACCESS:** This category describes the most difficult type of road encountered on the way to the site. Road conditions are subject to change. Regardless of what this guidebook indicates, if the road appears to be more difficult than for what you and your vehicle are equipped, do not attempt it. Sometimes the difficult part is near the end of the route. You can often get within walking distance before the road becomes too rough. In the case of four-wheel-drive (4WD) roads, there is usually some scenic aspect that can be enjoyed by travelers not having a four-wheel-drive vehicle. In these cases, the extent of what can be seen by passenger car is usually discussed in the description of the site. The following list gives the possible entries for the ACCESS category and their meanings:

PAVED ROAD: These sites are accessible by any passenger car.

GOOD DIRT ROAD: This kind of road is generally passable in either wet or dry weather.

DIRT ROAD: This type of road is usually passable under dry conditions but can become very muddy and potentially impassable when thoroughly wet.

ROUGH DIRT ROAD: This type of road may contain potholes, bumps, ruts, rocks, stream crossings, and slight sideways tilts. It may be impassable when wet. Passenger cars that travel this kind of road need a careful driver and at least average ground clearance. Two-wheel-drive vehicles with good ground clearance, such as pick-up trucks, should have no trouble.

EASY 4WD: Access to these sites requires a four-wheel-drive vehicle. Roads of this type are too rough or steep for passenger cars. A two-wheel-

# KEY TO INFORMATION BLOCK

drive vehicle with good ground clearance, such as a pick-up truck, can sometimes negotiate these roads.

MODERATE 4WD: A four-wheel-drive vehicle is required to visit these sites. The driver may have to work a little to traverse this type of road.

DIFFICULT 4WD: These roads are not for beginners. A certain amount of four-wheel-drive experience and skill may be required to safely negotiate the road.

HIKE: A walk of over a half-mile is required to reach the site.

**FACILITIES:** Visitor facilities are listed under this heading.

**TIME NEEDED:** Indicated is the minimum time needed to visit the site. In general, this does not include access time needed to reach the scenic location. However, it will include some of the driving time if the access is part of enjoying the scenery of the specific site.

**BEST VISIT:** This entry gives the best, but not the only, time of year to visit the site. Here, "best" is a combination of ease of access, personal comfort, and optimal scenic quality. In years of heavy snowfall, some sites may be blocked until much later than is indicated. Light snow years may offer earlier access. Many sites are particularly beautiful during the last weeks of September and the first weeks of October when the aspens turn color. The entries in this category are generally self-explanatory, but there is sometimes implied information in their recommendations, as indicated below:

SPRING OR FALL: These sites may be uncomfortably hot in summer.

MIDSUMMER TO LATE SUMMER: This entry refers to sites whose access is often blocked by snow well into summer. These same locations are sometimes cut off by early snows in September. Mid-July is not an unusual date for the higher sites to become accessible.

EARLY SUMMER TO FALL: Snow often blocks these sites during winter.

JULY: Waterfalls are usually most spectacular during this month.

**BEST PHOTO:** This category recommends the best, but not the only, time of day to photograph the site. In this case, "best" is when the natural lighting is optimal to photograph some distinctive aspect of the scenery. This assumes, of course, that the weather is cooperating—which it often doesn't. It is typical for mountain skies to become cloudy during the late afternoon in Colorado, even on days that start out clear. This entry may cover a wide portion of the day if numerous photographic opportunities

# KEY TO INFORMATION BLOCK

exist. Possible entries are listed below with typical times pertaining to a long, midsummer's day:

EARLY MORNING: Sunrise to 9:00 AM.

MORNING: 8:00 AM to 11:00 AM.

MIDDAY: 10:00 AM to 2:00 PM.

AFTERNOON: 1:00 PM to 5:00 PM.

LATE AFTERNOON: 4:00 PM to sunset.

**ELEVATION:** This category gives the altitude of the site in feet above sea level.

**REFERENCE:** This category gives an easy-to-find location used in the directions. The reference can be a city, an intersection of two well-identified highways, a well-marked mountain pass, or sometimes the intersection of a highway with a state or county line. An attempt has been made to select reference locations that are not likely to change with time. Reference locations can be found on the state highway map issued by the state of Colorado as well as on most other varieties of Colorado state highway maps.

**MAP:** This category lists the most convenient maps for locating the site. This is generally the state highway map, a United States Forest Service visitor map, a United States Geological Survey topographical map, or a Bureau of Land Management (BLM) map. The state highway map is listed if it shows all roads necessary to get to the site, even if the site itself is not identified.

**USGS TOPO:** This category gives the United States Geological Survey topographical maps of the 7.5 or 15 minute series that include the site. Maps of the 7.5 minute series offer high resolution with a scale of 1:24,000, and maps of the 15 minute series offer a scale of 1:62,500. All of the maps listed in this category are from the Colorado index of available USGS maps. This entry contains the name of the map, either 7.5' or 15' notation to identify the series, and the date of release or latest revision.

**USGS COUNTY:** This lists the United States Geological Survey county series topographic maps that cover the site. This series offers good resolution at 1:50,000 scale.

# KEY TO INFORMATION BLOCK

**DIRECTIONS:** The directions section contains accurate instructions on how to find the site. The directions give a route that begins with, or includes, the reference location that is listed in the information block. All of the directions were gathered during visits to the individual sites and were rechecked in 1982. For the second edition, almost all sites were revisited in 1989.

Unfortunately, directions are sometimes subject to change. If you are trying to locate a site and find that road intersections, turns, and landmarks are not where the instructions indicate, you will have to do your own navigation to reach that location. The maps supplied should prove handy in this case. If the access has been denied because it crosses private land, please do not attempt to approach the site by trespassing.

Cumulative mileages in the directions (enclosed by brackets: "< >") are given with respect to a beginning reference location. In general, distances are measured from the middle of locations. This applies to small towns, landmarks, tunnels, and the like. When this is not the case, the directions will indicate that the mileage refers to the beginning, end, entrance, or exit of some point of reference. For road intersections, distances are measured from the center of the intersection. Distances from highway interchanges (overpass or underpass) are measured from the middle of the roads where they cross each other.

The distances in the directions were measured by precalibrated odometer readings during visits to the sites. You may wish to calibrate your own odometer against mile-markers found on all Colorado interstate highways. Mileages that contain a decimal point and a tenths digit are intended to be accurate to the nearest tenth of a mile. Some sites are so well marked and so hard to miss that more casual directions are given.

# MAPS

Each item contains one or more maps for use with the directions to locate the site. These maps may also be handy for exploring some of the surrounding area not specifically discussed in the text. The source maps used sometimes show roads that are no longer accessible or passable. Even though an indicated road may still exist, its condition may have changed, making access either less or more difficult than the map shows. New roads may not be shown at all. Property ownership may have changed, resulting in reduced access. All of this depends on when the base maps used in this guide were last updated by the originating agency. The possibility of these variations should be taken into account.

The maps listed for each site cover only a small area and are intended to be used with the district map which is provided at the beginning of each district grouping of scenic sites. These district maps show the location of all the nearby sites included in a sizable portion of the state. A state map showing the location of all items in this book appears at the end of this chapter. A companion state highway map may be useful for navigation while on the road, and topographic maps with a high degree of resolution should be used as navigation aids to sites that require extensive hiking.

Maps included in this guide are excerpts from larger maps produced by state or federal government agencies. A scale indicator is given on each map. True north is always toward the top of the page unless otherwise indicated. The courtesy line at the bottom of each map identifies the originating government agency and implies which map key should be used to identify the meaning of the black and white symbols used on that map. These map keys follow this section and are arranged according to the originating map agency. No key is needed for maps generated by the National Park Service (NPS) and other agencies that use self-explanatory symbols.

# MAP OVERPRINT KEY

All maps used in this guide are overprinted with information in red to aid in finding the route to the site. The overprint symbols are:

■ Reference location used in directions

 Vehicular route

▲ Vista, overlook, or point of interest

------ Foot trail

★ Scenic item

⊢ 1 M ⊣ Scale of miles

# USDA FOREST SERVICE MAP KEY

LEGEND

| | | | |
|---|---|---|---|
| ▬▬▬▬▬ | National Forest Boundary | △ | Recreation Site |
| ▬ ▬ ▬ | Adjacent National Forest Boundary | △ | Recreation Site other than Forest Service |
| — — - — | County Boundary Line | 🎿 | Ski Area |
| — · — · — | Reservation Boundary | ▲ | Observation Site |
| ⠿⠿⠿⠿⠿ | Wilderness or Special Area Boundary | ◆ | Point of Interest |
| (70) | Interstate Highway | ● | Visitors Center |
| (285) | U.S. Highway | ▪ | House, Cabin or other Building |
| (9) | State Highway | ⌣ | Dam |
| [112] | Forest Route | ○ | Well |
| ▬▬▬▬▬ | Paved Road | | Water Well |
| ▬▬▬▬▬ | All Weather Road | —++-++— | Railroad Tunnel |
| ▬▬▬▬▬ | Dirt Road | | National Park or Monument |
| === ==≠=== 4WD | Primitive Road and Four Wheel Drive | | (Land ownership within boundary not shown)<br>National Recreation Area |
| ▬▬■▬▬ 215 | Freeway with Interchange | | State Land<br>(Permission required to enter) |
| — — — — — | Trail | | Arapaho National Forest Land |
| ♣ | District Ranger Station | | Adjacent National Forest Land |
| ♠ | Forest Service Station | | BLM Land |
| ✗ | Mine, Quarry or Gravel Pit | | |

Supervisors Headquarters, Fort Collins, Colorado

TOWNSHIP AND SECTION LINE CLASSIFICATION

——— Surveyed, location reliable

—— —— Surveyed, location approximate

— — — — Unsurveyed (Bureau of Land Management protraction)

*Courtesy of USDA Forest Service*

# BUREAU OF LAND MANAGEMENT MAP KEY

## MAP SYMBOLS

| Feature | Symbol | Feature | Symbol | Feature | Symbol | Feature | Symbol | Feature | Symbol |
|---|---|---|---|---|---|---|---|---|---|
| District Bdy | ———— | Road All Weather | Divided ═══ | Principal Access | Divided ═══ | Buildings | . ∙ ∙ | Towns and Cities | ◼ |
| Nat'l or State | — — — — | Road Seasonal Use | ═ ═ ═ ═ | | | Buildings (Abandoned) | ∘ ∘ ∘ | River or Large Stream | |
| | | Road "Jeep" Type "Primitive" | — ∙ — ∙ — | Road Interchange | —○— | BLM Office | ⌂ | Stream | |
| Continental Divide | — — — | Trail | — — — — | Rest Area | ═○═ | School | ⌂ | Large Dam | |
| County | — — — | Railroad Double Track | ——│—— | | | Church | ⌂ | Reservoir or Retention Dam | |
| Land Grant | — ∙ ∙ — | Railroad Single Track | ——│—— | | | Radio Installation | ⌂ | Lake or Pond | |
| Miscellaneous (Res., etc.) | — ∙ — | Glacier | ◌ | Levee or Dike | ······· | Fire Lookout (Primary) | ⓐ | Intermittent Lake or Pond | |
| Park (State, County or Local) | — — — — | Road Bridge | )⊨( | Corral | ⊂ | Fire Lookout (Secondary) | ⓐ | Dry Lake or Pond | |
| Township and Range | Surveyed ——— Protracted _ | Railroad Bridge | )⊨( | Recreation Site | △ | Fire Tool Cache | ⌂ | Marsh | |
| Section | Surveyed ——— Protracted_ _ | Foot Bridge | )—( | Tanks -(label as to type) | ○ | Shelter | ▢ | Spring | O→ |
| Sec., Status Subdivision | ———— | Ferry | )∙( | Oil or Gas Wells | ◊ | Cliff Dwelling | ⊓ | Improved Spring | O→→ |
| Section Identification | 6  ∷ | Road Ford | )⊨( | Mine or Quarry | ✕ | Ruins  Small / Large | ▢ Ruins / Ruins | Well | ○ |
| State Plane Coordinates And Zone | 1,500,000E | Trail Ford | —│—│— | US Mineral or Location Monument | ▲ | Cemetery | ⌂ CEM | Artesian Well | ⊙ |
| Boundary Monument | —⊙— | Road Tunnel | ═══ | Located Object (Labeled) | ⊙ | Sawmill | ▲ | Windmill | △ |
| Route Marker Interstate | ⬬ | Railroad Tunnel | ═══ | Triangulation Station | △ Dog | Airfield | ⊬ | Aqueduct Tunnel | →∙←∙← |
| Route Marker U.S. | ▢ | | | Bluffs or Cliffs | ∿∿ | | | Ditch or Canal | →∙—∙ |
| Route Marker State | ○ | Prominent Peak | ◇ | Prominent Ridge | ⌒ | Gaging Station | ⌂ | Aqueduct | →→→ |

*Courtesy of BLM*

# UNITED STATES GEOLOGIC SURVEY MAP KEY

Primary highway, hard surface .........................

Secondary highway, hard surface ......................

Light-duty road, hard or improved surface ............

Unimproved road .....................................

Road under construction, alinement known .............

Proposed road .......................................

Dual highway, dividing strip 25 feet or less ...........

Dual highway, dividing strip exceeding 25 feet ........

Trail ................................................

---

Railroad: single track and multiple track .............

Railroads in juxtaposition ............................

Narrow gage: single track and multiple track ..........

Railroad in street and carline ........................

Bridge: road and railroad ............................

Drawbridge: road and railroad .......................

Footbridge ..........................................

Tunnel: road and railroad ............................

Overpass and underpass ..............................

Small masonry or concrete dam ......................

Dam with lock .......................................

Dam with road ......................................

Canal with lock ......................................

---

Buildings (dwelling, place of employment, etc.).........

School, church, and cemetery .........................

Buildings (barn, warehouse, etc.) .....................

Power transmission line with located metal tower .......

Telephone line, pipeline, etc. (labeled as to type) .....

Wells other than water (labeled as to type) ............ oOil ..... oGas

Tanks: oil, water, etc. (labeled only if water) .......... • • ● ⊘Water

Located or landmark object; windmill ................. o .......... ↑

Open pit, mine, or quarry; prospect ................... ⋎ .......... x

Shaft and tunnel entrance ............................ ◼ ......... Y

---

Horizontal and vertical control station:

    Tablet, spirit level elevation ......................... BM △ 5653

    Other recoverable mark, spirit level elevation ........ △ 5455

Horizontal control station: tablet, vertical angle elevation VABM △ 95/9

    Any recoverable mark, vertical angle or checked elevation △ 3775

Vertical control station: tablet, spirit level elevation ..... BM X 957

    Other recoverable mark, spirit level elevation ........ X 954

Spot elevation ..................... ................ x 7369   x 7369

Water elevation ..................................... 670   ⊢ ⋋

*Courtesy of USGS*

# UNITED STATES GEOLOGIC SURVEY MAP KEY

Boundaries: National . . . . . . . . . . . . . . . . . . . . . . . . . . . . . . . .

    State . . . . . . . . . . . . . . . . . . . . . . . . . . . . . . . . . . . . .

    County, parish, municipio . . . . . . . . . . . . . . . . . . . . . . . . .

    Civil township, precinct, town, barrio . . . . . . . . . . . . . . . .

    Incorporated city, village, town, hamlet . . . . . . . . . . . . . . .

    Reservation, National or State . . . . . . . . . . . . . . . . . . . . . .

    Small park, cemetery, airport, etc. . . . . . . . . . . . . . . . . . . .

    Land grant . . . . . . . . . . . . . . . . . . . . . . . . . . . . . . . . . . . .

Township or range line, United States land survey . . . . . .

Township or range line, approximate location . . . . . . . . . .

Section line, United States land survey . . . . . . . . . . . . . . .

Section line, approximate location . . . . . . . . . . . . . . . . . . .

Township line, not United States land survey . . . . . . . . . .

Section line, not United States land survey . . . . . . . . . . . .

Found corner: section and closing . . . . . . . . . . . . . . . . . . .

Boundary monument: land grant and other . . . . . . . . . . . .

Fence or field line . . . . . . . . . . . . . . . . . . . . . . . . . . . . . . . .

---

Index contour . . . . . . . .          Intermediate contour . .

Supplementary contour               Depression contours . .

Fill . . . . . . . . . . . . . .          Cut . . . . . . . . . . . . . .

Levee . . . . . . . . . . . . .          Levee with road . . . . . .

Mine dump . . . . . . . . . .         Wash . . . . . . . . . . . . .

Tailings . . . . . . . . . . . .         Tailings pond . . . . . . .

Shifting sand or dunes               Intricate surface . . . . .

Sand area . . . . . . . . . . .        Gravel beach . . . . . . . .

---

Perennial streams . . . . .          Intermittent streams . .

Elevated aqueduct . . . .            Aqueduct tunnel . . . . . .

Water well and spring . . . . . . .  Glacier . . . . . . . . . . . . .

Small rapids . . . . . . . . .        Small falls . . . . . . . . . .

Large rapids . . . . . . . . .        Large falls . . . . . . . . . .

Intermittent lake . . . . .           Dry lake bed . . . . . . . . .

Foreshore flat . . . . . . .          Rock or coral reef . . . .

Sounding, depth curve                Piling or dolphin . . . . .

Exposed wreck . . . . . . .           Sunken wreck . . . . . . . .

Rock, bare or awash; dangerous to navigation . . . . . . . . . .

---

Marsh (swamp) . . . . . . .           Submerged marsh . . . .

Wooded marsh . . . . . . .            Mangrove . . . . . . . . . .

Woods or brushwood . .               Orchard . . . . . . . . . . . .

Vineyard . . . . . . . . . . .         Scrub . . . . . . . . . . . . . .

Land subject to
controlled inundation                Urban area . . . . . . . . .

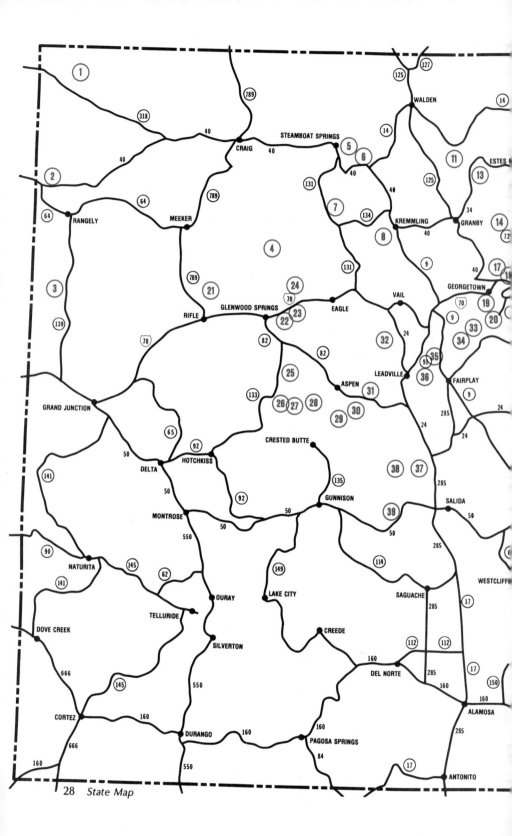

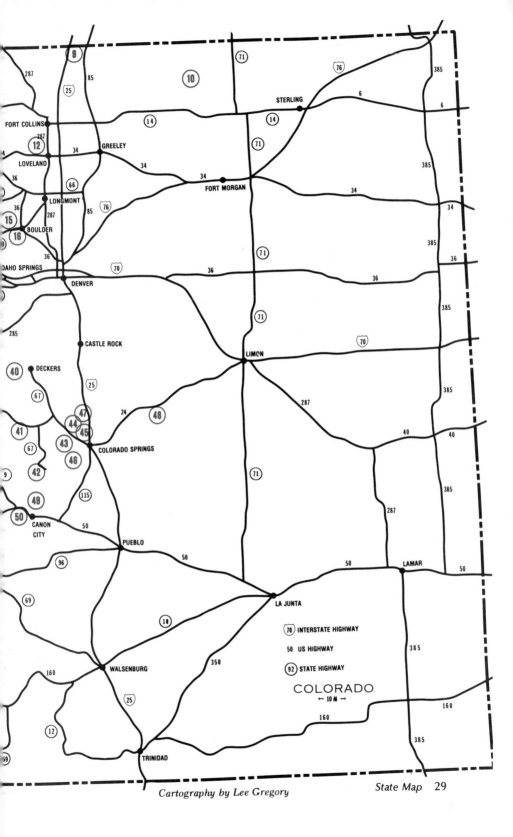

COLORADO

⌐ 10 M ⌐

70 INTERSTATE HIGHWAY

50 US HIGHWAY

92 STATE HIGHWAY

*Cartography by Lee Gregory*

# NORTHWEST DISTRICT

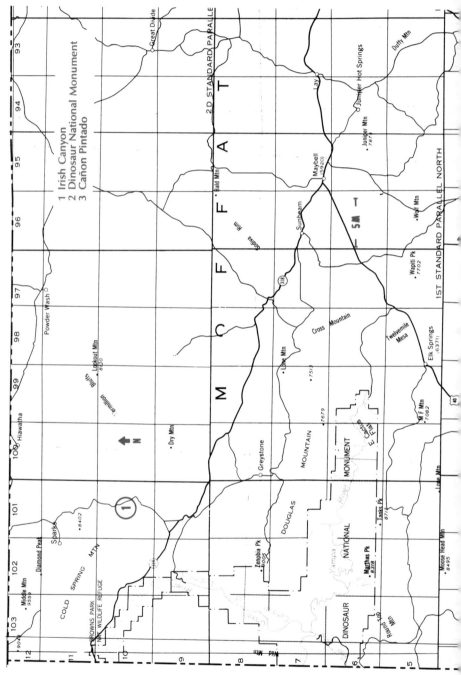

1 Irish Canyon
2 Dinosaur National Monument
3 Cañon Pintado

# NORTHWEST DISTRICT

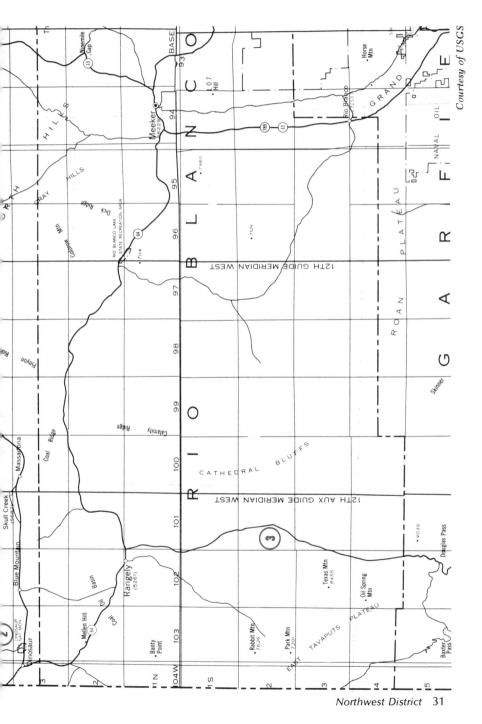

# 1  IRISH CANYON

TYPE: Plateau Scenery/Geologic/Historic
ADMINISTRATION: BLM land
QUALITY: Very scenic
ACCESS: Good dirt road
FACILITIES: Primitive campground/Picnic tables/Toilet
TIME NEEDED: One hour
BEST VISIT: Spring or fall
BEST PHOTO: Morning
ELEVATION: 6,101 feet (at petroglyphs)
REFERENCE: Maybell
MAP: State highway map
BLM Canyon of Lodore 1:100,000
USGS TOPO: Irish Canyon 7.5' (1966)
USGS COUNTY: Moffat County Sheet 1 of 7 (1975)

The history of Irish Canyon has the flavor of the Old West. Its name is attributed to three Irishmen who robbed a saloon in Rock Springs and later stopped in the canyon to consume some of their spoils. The canyon led to Browns Park (south of Cold Spring Mountain), whose isolation provided an ideal hideout for Butch Cassidy and his Wild Bunch, Tom Horn, and other notorious outlaws. In fact, an agreement was made among the group of outlaws to form the Wild Bunch, originally named the Train Robbers Syndicate by Cassidy, in Browns Park on August 18, 1896.

Irish Canyon, formed by uplifting and faulting, is a north-south incision across the sloping eastern end of Cold Spring Mountain. The southern mouth of the canyon is at 6,101 feet; its northern end is at 6,657. There is a high point of 6,680 feet in the floor of the canyon near the north end. This means that drainage starts at this point and empties through both the canyon's northern and southern entrances. This same characteristic—a divide with oppositely flowing drainages inside a canyon—is shared with Unaweep Canyon south of Grand Junction and is considered a geological rarity. Irish Canyon runs parallel to Vermilion Creek (to the east), which provides a major drainage path from regions north and east of the canyon to the Green River in Browns Park.

At the southern mouth of the canyon, a layer of sandstone is soon displaced by a lower layer of deep red to purple rock, which forms the high walls and the floor of the canyon at its deepest point. This colorful material is Uinta Mountain Red Creek quartzite, which underlies all of the Uinta Mountain region in both Colorado and Utah. Quartzite is sedimentary sandstone that has been subjected to heat and geologic pressures that caused the sand grains to fuse in a metamorphic process. The deep red coloration of the rock is due to iron oxides and other minerals contained between the quartz grains before this transformation process began. This hardened layer, up to 20,000 feet thick below the surface, represents some of the oldest exposed rocks in Colorado: 2.3 billion years as determined by radiometric dating. Above the

# 1 IRISH CANYON

The white rock of Limestone Ridge towers above the deep reddish-purple quartzite which forms the lower walls and floor of Irish Canyon.

The surface of this square sandstone boulder near the southern mouth of Irish Canyon exhibits several Fremont culture petroglyphs.

# 1  IRISH CANYON

red layer on the west canyon wall is a bold white layer that rises to an altitude of over 7,600 feet, forming the top of Limestone Ridge. As you continue into the straighter portion of the canyon, you make a transition back into the sandstones that overlay the Red Creek quartzite. The sandstone through the rest of the canyon offers a variety of colors including brown, yellow, tan, white, and gold. Near the north end is a primitive campground with three sites, each having one picnic table and a fire ring. Leaving Cold Spring Mountain through the north entrance of the canyon takes you back onto the relatively flat but canyon-cut plateau land of northwest Colorado. The road continues north to the Wyoming border and on to Rock Springs.

Just before entering the canyon from the south, there is a small turnout on the east side of the road. The turnout offers a single picnic table and a BLM register containing a map of the area and a short history of Irish Canyon. From here, a short foot trail leads to an isolated square sandstone block. Petroglyphs appear on both the side and top of this boulder, an uncommon occurrence. A petroglyph is Indian rock art that has been pecked, chiselled, or scraped into the surface of a rock. It differs from a pictograph in that it contains no pigments for coloration. A stain known as "desert varnish" darkens the surface of many sandstone rocks. Petroglyphs are most often cut into this smooth, dark layer to expose the lighter hues underneath. The characteristic shape of the figures on the top of the rock indicate that they are most likely of Fremont origin. This culture was active in northwest Colorado from around A.D. 800 to 1100. The more natural renderings on the side of the boulder may have been the more recent work of the Ute Indians. Irish Canyon may have been used in antiquity for big game drives. Please help protect these treasures by not touching or damaging them in any way.

**DIRECTIONS:** Proceed northwest on Colorado 318 (paved) from its junction <0.0> with US 40 just west of Maybell. A sign soon indicates that there are no services for the next 50 miles; be sure you have enough fuel before attempting to visit this area. Turn right (north) at a junction <41.5> with a gravel road marked by a sign indicating this turn for Rock Springs, Wyoming. There is also a sign at this intersection indicating a turn here for Irish Canyon (4 miles), Cold Spring Mountain Access (18 miles), and Rock Spring (76 miles). Continue to a pullout <45.8> on the right (east) side of the road. Here, at the mouth of Irish Canyon, is a picnic table, a small BLM register, and a short, log-lined foot trail leading to some petroglyphs with their own information sign. Continue north on the gravel road to a point <46.7> in the canyon well suited for photography. Continue past a primitive campground <49.7> with three picnic tables and fire rings to reach the northern end of the canyon <50.7>. Be sure to visit the Gates of Lodore (Dinosaur National Monument—site 2) while in this part of the district.

# 1 IRISH CANYON

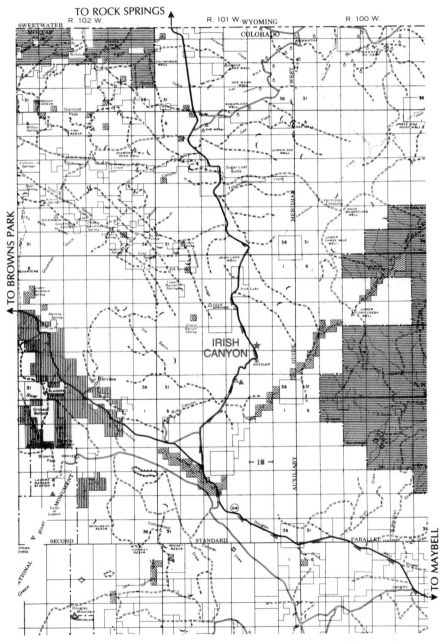

Courtesy of BLM

# 2  DINOSAUR NATIONAL MONUMENT

TYPE: Plateau Scenery/Geologic/Historic/
Paleontologic/Archaeologic
ADMINISTRATION: National Monument
QUALITY: Superbly scenic
ACCESS: Paved road
FACILITIES: Visitor centers/Campgrounds/Picnic grounds
TIME NEEDED: Two days
BEST VISIT: Spring or fall
BEST PHOTO: Morning (Gates of Lodore, Echo Park)
Afternoon (Harpers Corner)
ELEVATION: 7,440 feet (Harpers Corner)
REFERENCE: Dinosaur
MAP: State highway map
USGS TOPO: Dinosaur National Monument (1966) 1:62,500
USGS COUNTY: Moffat County Sheet 1 of 7 (1975)
Moffat County Sheet 5 of 7 (1975)

Its name implies that this monument has something to do with dinosaurs, and it does. It also has the finest sandstone canyon scenery in the state, archaeological sites, and an interesting contemporary history. The best place to start a visit is Monument Headquarters, where information concerning the monument as well as road conditions and specific directions to any point within the park can be obtained. Another place to begin is the Dinosaur Quarry Visitor Center in Utah, which can also supply this information.

The scenic drive north from the Monument Headquarters takes the visitor to the heart of canyon country within the park. Many scenic overlooks are available along this route, which ends at the Harpers Corner parking lot. A foot trail continues from there to an overlook (look for fossils under your feet) high above Whirlpool Canyon to the west and Echo Park to the east. This is the single best viewpoint in all of northern Colorado. The vista is unobstructed in all directions and follows the landscape down to the river level, a dramatic 2,350 feet below. The Green River cuts its way through the ancient, deep red quartzite from the north, and the Yampa winds its way through the bright white sandstone to the east. The two rivers meet in Echo Park, just east of Steamboat Rock. Their path continues south a short distance, makes an abrupt 180-degree turn, and flows north again around Steamboat Rock, a slender, sheer-walled, 750-foot tall sandstone peninsula. The river makes a gradual turn north of the overlook and then continues west toward Utah through Whirlpool Canyon.

The Gates of Lodore, though isolated, are an easily accessible part of the monument. This name was given in honor of Southey's poem "How the Waters Come Down at Lodore" by a member of the John Wesley Powell expedition of 1869. The Green River exits from the Flaming Gorge area of Utah and ambles across the wide, flat valley of Browns Park. In the gentle

Echo Park as seen from Harpers Corner overlook is one of the best views in northern Colorado.

A ranger answers questions about the origin of fossilized dinosaur bones in this layer of sandstone at the Dinosaur Quarry Visitor Center.

STATE OF COLORADO

Harpers Corner overlook offers this fantastic view of Whirlpool Canyon.

# 2  DINOSAUR NATIONAL MONUMENT

The great walls of the Gates of Lodore rise 2,000 feet above the Green River as it plunges into Douglas Mountain.

# 2  DINOSAUR NATIONAL MONUMENT

terrain of Browns Park, the river makes an abrupt and unexpected turn to the south and dives into Douglas Mountain. As the river enters the mountain, it cuts a narrow, vertical-walled canyon through the deeply colored Uinta Mountain quartzite. In a brief span, the walls of this enclosure rise from the flat terrain of Browns Park to over 2,000 feet at the edge of the mountain. This dramatic mouth of the canyon is truly spectacular—a much overused term in most cases, but hardly sufficient for this location. A nature trail at the end of the access road to the Gates of Lodore takes the visitor to the top of a bluff for a magnificent view of this scenic wonder.

The Dinosaur Quarry, in Utah, is a unique building constructed around a very special formation of sandstone. This layer of sediment was once a sandbar on a river that coursed through this vicinity about 140 million years ago. Bones of 10 species of dinosaur have been found in this 12-foot-thick layer. The cause of death of these dinosaurs is unknown, but somehow they ended up in the river and were deposited on an inside turn where the current probably slowed. The remains of these reptiles were probably chewed on a bit by scavengers, who helped scatter the bones. Through the ages, the bones that were completely buried by the sand have become fossilized, and the sand itself is now sandstone. Bones are no longer removed from this strata, but are exposed in their natural matrix within the sandstone for viewing.

**DIRECTIONS:** Monument Headquarters are located on US 40 at a well-marked turn just 1.9 miles east of the intersection of US 40 and Colorado 64 in the town of Dinosaur. There is a scenic drive (paved) that leads north from the Headquarters to the center of the canyon district of the monument at Harpers Corner. From the Headquarters, proceed north—stopping for all of the scenic points, of course—on the scenic drive for a little over 25 miles to a junction with a primitive dirt road (not suitable for large, heavy vehicles or trailers) to the right (east). This side road, 14 miles long, drops to a primitive campground in beautiful Echo Park at the confluence of the Green and Yampa rivers. Cars with good ground clearance should be able to reach Echo Park under favorable weather conditions; inquire at the Headquarters about the condition of this road. All of the primitive roads in the monument are impassable when wet. Continuing north on the pavement from this intersection for another 6 miles brings you to the Harpers Corner trailhead. The mostly level foot trail to the overlook is a two-mile round trip.

The Dinosaur Quarry Visitor Center can be reached by heading west on US 40 from the town of Dinosaur to Jensen, Utah, a distance of 22 miles. Turn right (north) onto Utah 149 at a well-marked intersection. Follow this paved road for a distance of 7 miles to the Visitor Center parking area.

The Gates of Lodore are in the isolated northern bounds of the monument. From the town of Dinosaur, proceed east on US 40 for a distance of 59 miles to its intersection with Colorado 318. There are no services for 50 miles on 318, so be sure you have enough fuel. Turn left (northwest)

# 2 DINOSAUR NATIONAL MONUMENT

at this intersection <0.0> and follow Colorado 318 (paved) to a junction <39.9> with a good gravel road to the left marked by a sign indicating Gates of Lodore. (See the map on page 35.) Turn here and continue to the next junction <40.5> with a gravel road to the right. Make a right turn here and continue straight at the next intersection <45.2> with a gravel road to the right (return to State 318). Continue past the Dinosaur National Monument Gates of Lodore sign <47.7>, past the Ranger Station <48.3>, and through the campground to a parking area <49.6> at the end of the road. From here, a nature trail climbs the hill to the south culminating in a truly spectacular view. Be sure to visit Irish Canyon (site 1) while you are in this part of the northwest district.

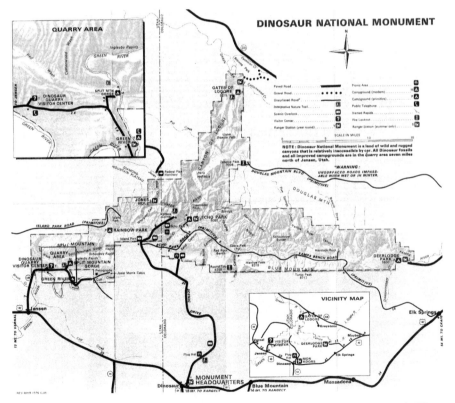

*Courtesy of NPS*

# 3 CAÑON PINTADO

**TYPE:** Plateau Scenery/Archaeologic/Historic
**ADMINISTRATION:** BLM land
**QUALITY:** Scenic
**ACCESS:** Paved road
**FACILITIES:** Picnic table/Shelter
**TIME NEEDED:** Half hour
**BEST VISIT:** Spring or fall
**BEST PHOTO:** Morning
**ELEVATION:** 5,920 feet (at pictographs)
**REFERENCE:** Rangely
**MAP:** State highway map
BLM Douglas Pass 1:100,000
**USGS TOPO:** White Coyote Draw 7.5' (1964)
**USGS COUNTY:** Rio Blanco County Sheet 5 of 6 (1975)

Cañon Pintado, Spanish for painted canyon, was the name given by Franciscan Fathers Francisco Atanasio Dominguez and Silvestre Velez de Escalante to what is today called Douglas Creek Canyon. The two men were leaders of a 1776 expedition in search of a convenient route from Santa Fe, New Mexico, to the Spanish settlements and missions of California. By request of the governor of New Mexico, the expedition was to find a land route linking these Spanish strongholds, explore the little-known Spanish frontier between these two areas, and consider opportunities to subdue the less-than-cooperative Hopi Indians. The fathers left Santa Fe on July 29, 1776, accompanied by six other men, including Captain Miera, who had been trained in the use of the astrolabe, an instrument to chart their progress.

Without the aid of a guide, the expedition maneuvered generally north until it came upon the Dolores River in Colorado. The party followed the river until steep-walled canyons forced them to go cross-country in the arid lands of the western Colorado plateau. It was fortunate for Dominguez and Escalante that they were able to secure the services of two Ute Indians near the Uncompahgre River who led them north over Grand Mesa, across the Colorado River, and north across the Roan Plateau, just east of Douglas Pass. The party then dropped into a canyon drained by Douglas Creek, which flowed north.

The September 9, 1776, entry in Escalante's diary noted that the group followed a well-worn trail that paralleled Douglas Creek through a canyon. They continued to a point where they discovered crude paintings depicting three shields and the blade of a spear on the canyon wall. Further down the canyon, they encountered another painting bearing the likeness of two men in combat. The expedition continued north until they encountered the White River, which they named El Rio San Clemente. Here they made camp, and it was reported in Father Escalante's diary that this was the only habitable location in the area. The present-day town of Rangely near this

# 3 CAÑON PINTADO

These Fremont culture pictographs were discovered by Dominguez and Escalante during their 1776 expedition of the American Southwest.

A closer study of the pictographs on the left side of the full panel reveals the detail and pigment variation used in the creation of this rock art.

# 3  CAÑON PINTADO

spot is the only settlement in the region. The party continued west along the White River toward Utah. With the end of summer drawing near, the fathers gave up their quest and returned to Santa Fe through southern Utah and across Arizona. Although their goal was not achieved, their exploration added much to Spain's knowledge of her holdings and was the first time Europeans had seen and recorded a large portion of the Southwest.

The paintings, already ancient when discovered by Dominguez and Escalante, are a form of Indian rock art known as pictographs, renderings usually made on smooth, light-colored rock with pigments derived from local minerals, colorful clays, and, in some cases, organic material such as blood. Most pictographs are found on rock surfaces protected from the elements, usually by a rock overhang. The pictographs in this canyon are probably the work of the Fremont culture, which existed in this area from A.D. 800 to 1100. One of the figures of this panel has been identified as Kokopelli, the humpbacked flute player, who is an important spiritual being to the present-day Hopi Indians of Arizona. The Hopi are probably the descendants of the Anasazi, an advanced culture of pueblo dwellers who dominated the Southwest. The Fremont and Anasazi peoples have left a diverse and copious rock art heritage throughout the Southwest. Though this art may have been some type of graffiti, it is much more likely to be religious in nature: visual offerings to benevolent and powerful spirits, whose help was needed for survival in the desert. These pictographs are an important part of our cultural heritage. Please do not touch or damage them in any way. Additional information about area rock art can be found at the Rangely Museum (434 W. Main St.).

**DIRECTIONS:** From Rangely, head east on Colorado 64 toward its junction with Colorado 139 just beyond the eastern edge of town. Half a mile before (west of) this junction, there is a turnout on the north side of the highway. The turnout has a single picnic table under a sunshade next to a historical marker and informative sign about the Dominguez—Escalante expedition camp near this spot. From the intersection <0.0> of Colorado 64 and 139, turn right (south) and continue to a picnic table and shelter <15.9> on the left (east) side of the road at mile-marker 56. Directly across the road on the west wall of the canyon are the pictographs with a small informative sign near their base.

For an alternative route starting at Grand Junction, proceed west on Interstate 70 to the Loma exit (exit 15). Take this exit and continue north through Loma on Colorado 139. Proceed on this road to Douglas Pass where pleasant views south toward Grand Junction are available. From the summit <0.0> of Douglas Pass, continue north to the turnout <20.9> on the east side of the road at mile-marker 56.

# 3 CAÑON PINTADO

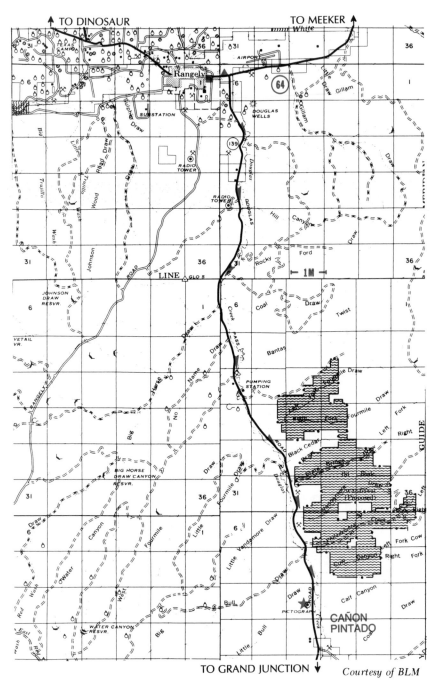

Courtesy of BLM

# STEAMBOAT SPRINGS DISTRICT

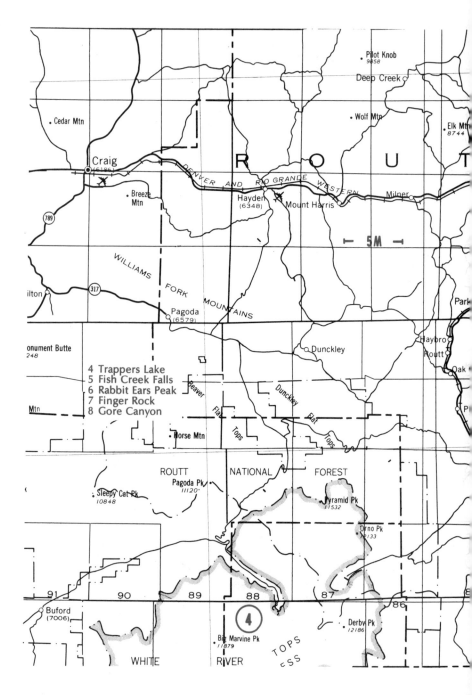

4 Trappers Lake
5 Fish Creek Falls
6 Rabbit Ears Peak
7 Finger Rock
8 Gore Canyon

# STEAMBOAT SPRINGS DISTRICT

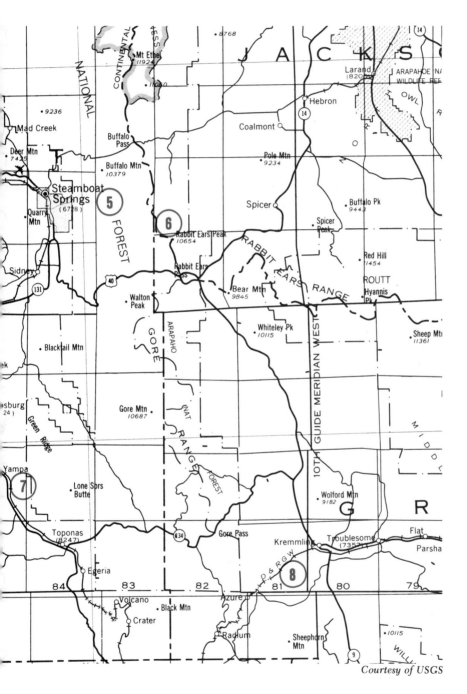

Courtesy of USGS

# 4 TRAPPERS LAKE

TYPE: Plateau Scenery
ADMINISTRATION: White River National Forest
QUALITY: Very scenic
ACCESS: Good dirt road
FACILITIES: Campgrounds
TIME NEEDED: One hour
BEST VISIT: Early summer to fall
BEST PHOTO: Afternoon
ELEVATION: 9,627 feet (lake surface)
REFERENCE: Meeker
MAP: State highway map
White River National Forest visitor map
USGS TOPO: Trappers Lake 7.5' (1977)
Devil's Causeway 7.5' (1977)
USGS COUNTY: Garfield County Sheet 1 of 5 (1975)

Trappers Lake, situated at the headwaters of the White River, is one of Colorado's most serenely scenic spots. The backdrop, known as the Amphitheater, of this 313-acre lake affords it a unique beauty. To the south, a high rim curves to conform with the inlaid setting of the lake. The summit of this level-topped enclosure stands more than 1,700 feet above the surface of the lake. The green vegetation on its otherwise gray slopes provides a colorful complement to the deep blue hues of the foreground waters. This location invites one to sit and enjoy the quiet natural dignity of the wilderness.

It was this site that spawned the notion within the National Forest Service of protecting wilderness areas. Trappers Lake is located in the Flat Tops region, the highest section of the White River Plateau. This area was first protected within the bounds of the 1.2-million-acre White River Plateau Timberland Reserve established by President Harrison in 1891. This was the first such preservation in Colorado and only the second of its kind in the entire nation. It was not until 1905 that these timber reserves were reorganized into national forests and were transferred to the jurisdiction of the Department of Agriculture. A decade or so later, the Forest Service began to notice the arrival of more tourists and visitors to the forest lands under their control. Having minimal experience in accomodating these activities, the Forest Service resolved to plan for future recreational development. One of the first sites under such consideration was Trappers Lake.

Arthur H. Carhart, a landscape architect by profession, was hired in 1919 to advise in these development plans. After preparing a recreation plan for the San Isabel National Forest in central Colorado, he traveled to Trappers Lake to study the situation. Before his arrival, the proposed plan was to establish sites for summer cabins and to lay out a road encircling the lake, but Carhart, impressed by the natural beauty of the lake in its unspoiled condition, made the radical recommendation that the lake be left in its original

# 4 TRAPPERS LAKE

The Amphitheater forms part of the scenic background of Trappers Lake.

# 4 TRAPPERS LAKE

setting, with any development taking place at least a half-mile from its shore. This was the first recommendation within the Forest Service that certain holdings could best serve the recreational needs of the public when left in their wild state. Finding it nearly impossible to redirect the inertia of a federal agency, Carhart lost patience with the lack of interest in wilderness preservation and resigned his position in 1922. His stay was not entirely without effect, however. Influenced by Carhart's determination, the head of the Forest Service district office in Denver abolished the plan to construct a road around the lake and refused to grant private homesite applications.

Meanwhile, a conference between Carhart and Aldo Leopold of the Albuquerque Forest Service office later led to the establishment, in 1924, of the nation's first wilderness preserve within Gila National Forest in New Mexico. Other such areas were designated informally on an office-by-office basis until 1929, when uniform policies were established. At that time, the Flat Tops Primitive Area was officially designated but still did not contain Trappers Lake. Not until 1975 were the boundaries expanded to include the lake, and the district was reclassified as a wilderness area.

Despite this long delay in formal preservation, little development has been allowed within sight of the lake. The biggest distraction to be seen today is a fisherman in his unpowered boat angling for Colorado's native high-altitude cutthroat trout. A regular maze of trails encircles the lake and crisscrosses the wilderness area in all directions. One trail leads east from the lake past Little Trapper Lake to the top of the Chinese Wall, visible east of the Trappers Lake area from many locations. After several miles, this trail ends at Devil's Causeway, a quarter-mile-long rock sliver that stands a

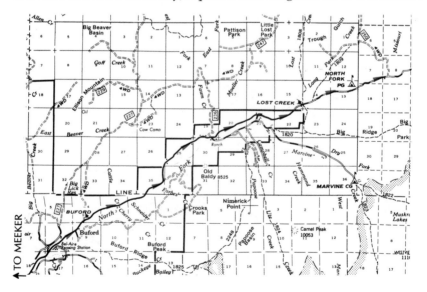

# 4 TRAPPERS LAKE

thousand feet above the surrounding terrain yet is barely wide enough for a person to cross. Numerous other lakes are interspersed with the forest of this generally flat plateau highland. A substantial annual rainfall ensures lush vegetation throughout the region.

**DIRECTIONS:** Proceed east from Meeker a short distance on Colorado 13 (also designated Colorado 789) to a point where the highway starts to curve left and head north. Here, there is a junction with a paved road to the right marked by a sign identifying turns for Craig (straight arrow), Buford (right arrow), and Trappers Lake (right arrow). Turn right at this intersection <0.0> and follow this road east past Buford <20.5> to the end of the pavement <30.3>. Continue straight on the good graveled road that takes up where the pavement ends to a junction with a road to the right marked by a sign indicating Trappers Lake. Turn right at this intersection <38.7> and follow the good dirt road (Forest Road 205) to a junction <46.3> with a road to the right which crosses a bridge. This intersection is marked by a sign indicating Trappers Lake Outlet Parking (¼ mile straight), Trappers Lake Campground (¾ mile right), Wall Lake Trailhead (1 mile right), and Scotts Bay Parking Area (1 mile right). Continue straight to the Trappers Lake Outlet Parking area <46.6>. For a quarter-mile walk to the lake edge, take the trail marked by a sign where it leaves the parking area. This vantage point offers good photographic opportunities. Various other access points to the lake can be reached by turning right at the previous intersection. There is a short walk from each of these parking areas to the lake.

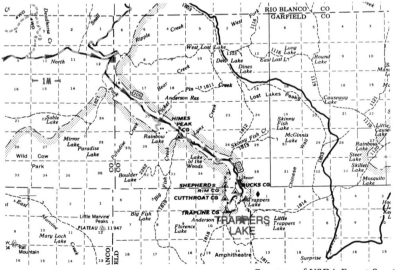

*Courtesy of USDA Forest Service*

# 5   FISH CREEK FALLS

TYPE: Mountain Scenery
ADMINISTRATION: Private land/Routt National Forest
QUALITY: Very scenic
ACCESS: Good dirt road
FACILITIES: Rest rooms/Picnic area
TIME NEEDED: Half hour
BEST VISIT: July
BEST PHOTO: Afternoon
ELEVATION: 7,560 feet (top of falls)
REFERENCE: Steamboat Springs
MAP: Routt National Forest visitor map
USGS TOPO: Steamboat Springs 7.5' (1969)
USGS COUNTY: Routt County Sheet 4 of 5 (1975)

Fish Creek Falls, a short distance east of Steamboat Springs, is 5.5 miles west of the Continental Divide and is within the Pacific Ocean watershed. Two hundred feet high, this waterfall is located on Fish Creek near the western boundary of Routt National Forest. The falls drop over a nearly vertical cliff into a short but rugged little canyon. The drainage basin that supplies Fish Creek is boxed to the north by Buffalo Mountain (10,379 feet), to the south by Mount Werner (10,565 feet), and to the west by the Continental Divide along the Park Range (approximately 10,500 feet). Snow accumulation during the winter provides most of the moisture to Long Lake and the tributary streams that feed the South Fork of Fish Creek. The North Fork has its sources in streams from the Buffalo Pass area and from Lake Dinosaur. Fish Creek Reservoir feeds the Middle Fork, which joins the North Fork immediately south of Buffalo Mountain. This then joins the South Fork near the falls to complete Fish Creek. From here, the creek descends 720 feet over a distance of a few miles to its confluence with the Yampa River just south of Steamboat Springs.

The falls are usually at their best in July, the typical month of maximum snowmelt runoff. At its peak flow, Fish Creek is an absolute torrent as it crashes over the falls and fills the canyon below with frothy white water. Because the falls face west and slightly to the north, the best opportunity to see them in full, direct sunlight is in the midafternoon during the last weeks of June and early July. The large footbridge spanning Fish Creek just below the falls provides an ideal viewpoint. The trail that continues on the other side of this bridge follows Fish Creek for several miles to Long Lake, just below the Continental Divide. In addition, there are several other hiking trails in the surrounding areas of Routt National Forest. Access to the area is via paved and good gravel roads. Passenger cars should have no difficulty in reaching the parking area.

Nearby Steamboat Springs (elevation 6,728 feet) was founded in 1875 by homesteader James H. Crawford. The town name comes from a spring, located on a sharp bend of the Yampa River, whose venting steam sounded

# 5 FISH CREEK FALLS

A footbridge fills the foreground of this view of Fish Creek Falls from the trail.

# 5  FISH CREEK FALLS

like a steamboat under full power. This spring has since lost its voice, probably because of construction of a railway cut nearby, but still issues hot mineral water into the river. There are about 150 other springs in the area, some cool, some warm, with an average of around 75°F. Some of these springs produce heavily mineralized water and were once used for medicinal purposes by the Ute Indians of the region. Water heated deep below the surface follows a series of geological faults between the Precambrian rock forming the Park Range and the Mesozoic sediments steeply tilted in this vicinity. It then flows forth from Dakota sandstone at the surface. The heated subsurface water causes various minerals, especially calcium carbonate from limestone, to be dissolved and carried to the surface. As this water evaporates near the mouth of the spring, the calcium carbonate and other minerals are left behind to produce a gray formation known as travertine. The passageway of an extinct spring near the Yampa River forms Sulfur Cave, one of Colorado's most unusual caverns. Its interior is lined with crystals of sulfur deposited by mineral-laden water when the spring was active. At least two deaths have been attributed to toxic sulfur dioxide gas in this extremely dangerous cave.

**DIRECTIONS:** The directions to Fish Creek Falls begin in Steamboat Springs at the intersection of Lincoln Avenue (US 40) and Third Street near the east end of the older part of downtown. Turn north onto Third Street off US 40 at this intersection <0.0> and continue for one block to an intersection <0.05> with Oak Street at a four-way stop. A sign at this intersection indicates Fish Creek Falls to the right. Turn right onto Oak Street and continue in an easterly direction. Oak Street soon becomes Fish Creek Falls Road. Go straight at the intersection <1.3> where the pavement ends and a good gravel road continues. The road curves several times and ends in a large parking area <3.2>. A paved, wheelchair accessible path leads to a high overlook of the falls and to the restrooms and picnic area. You can continue downhill from the picnic area to the footbridge across Fish Creek. This is a good place to view the falls. Beyond the bridge, Long Lake Trail turns right (west) and starts to climb the hill to reach a level even with the top of the falls. The trail now parallels Fish Creek for six miles and gains over 2,000 feet on the way to Long Lake just below the Continental Divide. A short side trail leads to Upper Fish Creek Falls about a mile before Long Lake.

# 5 FISH CREEK FALLS

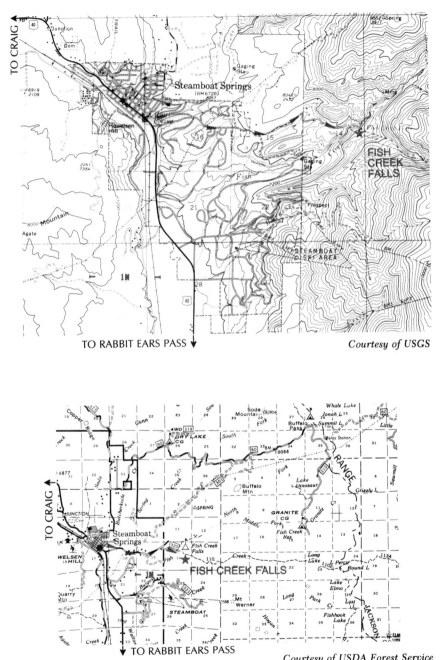

TO RABBIT EARS PASS ↓                         *Courtesy of USGS*

↓ TO RABBIT EARS PASS                 *Courtesy of USDA Forest Service*

# 6 RABBIT EARS PEAK

TYPE: Mountain Scenery/Geologic
ADMINISTRATION: Routt National Forest
QUALITY: Scenic
ACCESS: Paved road
FACILITIES: Nearby campgrounds and picnic areas
TIME NEEDED: Half hour
BEST VISIT: Early summer to fall
BEST PHOTO: Morning to midday
ELEVATION: 10,654 feet (summit)
REFERENCE: Steamboat Springs
MAP: State highway map
Routt National Forest visitor map
USGS TOPO: Rabbit Ears Peak 7.5' (1956)
USGS COUNTY: Jackson County Sheet 3 of 4 (1978)

The summit of Rabbit Ears Peak is the weathered remains of a volcanic plug, the result of a tube that once supplied molten material to the portal of an active volcano. When this volcano ceased activity, the molten material cooled and hardened into a shaft of granulate volcanic material bonded together with a reddish lava. The rock that once surrounded this tube eroded more easily than its contents, leaving the plug, separated into two independent pillars, standing about 100 feet above the terrain. Just east of the summit, Dakota sandstone is exposed at the surface where the sedimentary layers underlying North Park have been tilted by the uplift of the Park Range. The Park Range itself is composed of igneous granite and metamorphic gneiss and schist. The relatively level, though rolling, terrain where US 40 crosses the range is the result of glacial action during the Pleistocene period. At that time, the whole of the Park Range supported various icecaps, and glacial fingers pointed into the canyons to both the east and west.

Looking from the southwest, the viewer may wonder what sort of vivid imagination is required to derive the name Rabbit Ears, used since the earliest trappers and mountain men roamed the area, from this formation. One can observe two independent shafts of rock, but the proportions of these pillars gives them a stubby appearance, nothing like the tall, slender ears of a rabbit. This remains perplexing until Rabbit Ears Peak is viewed from the southeast. A proper vantage point shows that the easternmost pillar is itself split. The narrow cut extends about halfway down the pillar, giving the appearance of a pair of lengthy, narrow, almost touching ears attached to the head of a huge rabbit peeking over the brow of the hill. These ears can be seen from the middle of North Park all the way south to near Kremmling.

Three miles directly south of the peak is Rabbit Ears Pass, part of the Continental Divide at 9,426 feet. Drainage to the east of the pass ends in the Atlantic Ocean through the Platte, Missouri, and Mississippi rivers. The western drainage from the pass works its way to the Pacific Ocean via the Yampa, Green, and Colorado rivers. The old highway across Rabbit Ears

Separated volcanic pillars atop the mountain form the summit of Rabbit Ears Peak. A more easterly view of the right pillar shows a better silhouette of the rabbit's ears.

# 6 RABBIT EARS PEAK

Pass, since replaced by the present highway, was constructed in 1919 as part of the Victory Highway extending from Denver to Salt Lake City, Utah. Two miles east of Rabbit Ears Pass is Muddy Pass, the lowest pass on the Continental Divide within Colorado at 8,772 feet. Lieutenant John Charles Fremont used this pass to cross south from North Park into Middle Park in 1844 on one of his mapping expeditions through the state.

**DIRECTIONS:** Proceed southeast from Steamboat Springs on US 40 past the Steamboat ski area on Mount Werner to the left (east). Continue on US 40 beyond the intersection <0.0> with Colorado 131. US 40 begins to climb the Park Range and continues past the Ferndale Picnic Area <14.5> on the left (north) side of the road. A brief stop at the Yampa Valley Vista <14.7> offers sweeping views of the Yampa River basin to the south and west. Continue past Harrison Creek Picnic Ground <15.2> to the "west summit" of Rabbit Ears Pass <18.2>. A parking area is provided here. From this point, US 40 continues across the relatively level crown of the Park Range. Still proceeding east, go past Meadows Campground <19.4> and the Grand County line <23.5> to the junction <24.4> with a paved road to the left identified by a sign indicating Dumont Lake. Turn left (north) at this intersection and then right (east) onto old US 40 <24.5>. Continue on this paved road beyond the (closed) Dumont Campground turnoff <25.5> to the junction <25.9> with a dirt road. This road to the left is identified by a sign indicating Base Campground (4 miles left), End of Road (4 miles left), and Fishhook Lake (6 miles left). At this intersection a brass plaque set in stone identifies this location as Rabbit Ears Pass. Rabbit Ears Peak is two miles north and slightly to the east. For the adventurous, closer views of the peak are available from along this rough and often muddy road leading north from the marker. If you wish to hike or jeep toward the summit of the peak, follow this road north for a third of a mile, then turn right (east) and follow an old jeep road that winds its way to Rabbit Ears Peak over a total distance of three miles. The pavement continues beyond the marker a short distance to where the old highway ends.

Upon returning to US 40 <0.0>, you may wish to turn left and continue east to the present highway crossing of Rabbit Ears Pass <1.4> identified by a sign as part of the Continental Divide at an altitude of 9,426 feet. The parking area just east of the pass offers a good view of Rabbit Ears Peak. From here, the split in the eastern pillar can be seen to form the silhouette of a pair of rabbit's ears. The road continues past Muddy Pass Lake <4.0> to a junction <4.6> with Colorado 14 atop Muddy Pass, identified by a sign. Rabbit Ears Peak can also be seen from along Colorado 14 as it crosses the southern regions of North Park.

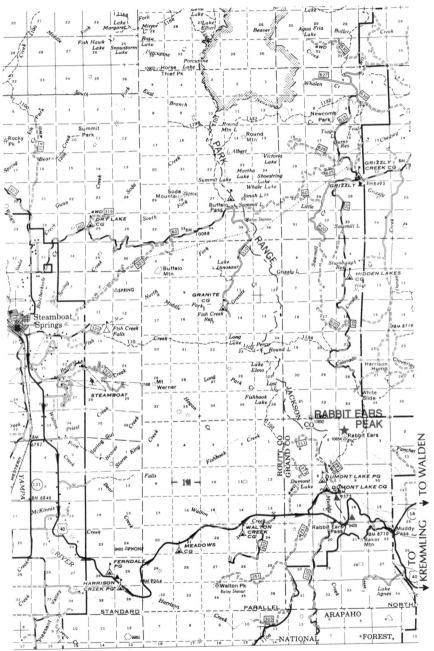

Courtesy of USDA Forest Service

# 7 FINGER ROCK

| | |
|---:|:---|
| **TYPE:** | Geologic Scenery |
| **ADMINISTRATION:** | BLM land/Private land |
| **QUALITY:** | Scenic |
| **ACCESS:** | Paved road |
| **FACILITIES:** | None |
| **TIME NEEDED:** | Quarter hour |
| **BEST VISIT:** | Spring to fall |
| **BEST PHOTO:** | Afternoon to late afternoon |
| **ELEVATION:** | 8,360 feet (top of formation) |
| **REFERENCE:** | Yampa |
| **MAP:** | State highway map |
| | Routt National Forest visitor map |
| **USGS TOPO:** | Trapper 7.5' (1972) |
| **USGS COUNTY:** | Routt County Sheet 5 of 5 (1975) |

Indian legend holds that a young warrior broke off his finger while wrestling with the god Manitou. The finger, left here on the ground, was turned to stone as a symbol of this struggle. A variation of this legend states that the warrior himself was turned to stone when he raised his finger in defiance of Manitou. It is believed by geologists that this spire is the remnant of a volcano formed from general volcanic activity in the area during Miocene and Oligocene times (20 to 35 million years ago). Finger Rock was once a conduit for molten lava that had forced its way through the surrounding sedimentary rock layers. When this activity ceased, the lava cooled inside the earth to form this volcanic plug. The erosion-resistant plug came into view as the surrounding soft sandstone eroded to the present surface over the millennia. This solitary shaft stands isolated from the surrounding terrain and is one of several volcanic formations along the eastern edge of the Yampa Valley. Finger Rock stands 350 feet above the valley floor between the towns of Yampa (an Indian word for a plant of the region with an edible root) and Toponas (an Indian word for sleeping lion, named after a nearby rock formation). The spire is located southwest of Gore Mountain at the western end of Gore Pass, which crosses the Gore Range.

Many features of the area include the Gore name. Sir St. George Gore, eighth baronet of Manor Gore in Ireland, was one of Colorado's colorful nineteenth-century characters. Lord Gore was an outdoorsman with a lust for the wholesale slaughter of big game in the name of sport. He was guided by Jim Bridger during the three years (1854-1857) of his exploits in Colorado, Wyoming, Montana, and North Dakota. Gore was usually accompanied by 40 men with their associated hounds, carts, wagons, and numerous camp luxuries. Nothing was left to chance; enough ammunition was brought from England to kill every living creature in the untamed American West. During these travels, over 2,000 buffalo, 1,600 elk and deer, and 100 bear were killed. Late in the summer of 1854, the group found its way from Fort Laramie on the Oregon Trail across the Medicine Bow Mountains into North

# 7  FINGER ROCK

Solitary Finger Rock stands 350 feet above the valley floor.

# 7 FINGER ROCK

Park and then across the Continental Divide at Muddy Pass into Middle Park.

It was from Middle Park, in the fall of 1854, that Bridger led Lord Gore into the valley of the Yampa near Finger Rock. The route was over a pass known only to Indians and a few mountain men. They discovered that a small band of Yampa Ute Indians occupied the valley. These Indians were friendly toward Bridger, having had previous trading business with him at Fort Bridger near the Green River. Chief White Eye of the Yampa Utes suggested that Bridger and Gore not continue their hunting party down the valley, as the enclosed game was the sole property of their tribe. Bridger guided the group back to Middle Park after exchanging gifts with the chief. Despite their hasty return, the journey over the thickly forested pass was through prime elk country and yielded several trophies. The entourage then returned to Fort Laramie at the close of the season.

Seven years later, Colorado was designated a territory, owing mostly to the gold rush that began in 1859. William Gilpin, first territorial governor, engaged the Central Overland, California, and Pike's Peak Express Company to locate a wagon road between Denver and Salt Lake City. Bridger was hired as guide to E. L. Berthoud, the company's chief engineer. As the expedition crossed the same pass previously used by Lord Gore to enter the Yampa Valley, Bridger suggested the crossing be named Gore Pass, and it was so recorded. Gore Pass was a trail by 1866 and a wagon road by 1874. The modern paved highway, Colorado 134, was opened in 1956. A brass plaque mounted at the summit of Gore Pass gives a brief biography of the legendary Lord Gore.

**DIRECTIONS:** From Steamboat Springs, proceed southeast on US 40 to its junction with Colorado 131. Turn right at this intersection and follow Colorado 131 south for 27 miles to the town of Yampa. The highway crosses a small river via a bridge <0.0> at the south end of town. A small white sign attached to the bridge identifies the river as the Yampa, despite the fact that it is actually the Bear River, which joins Chimney Creek just east of town to form the Yampa River. Continue south on the highway to Finger Rock <2.1> on the left (east) side of the road, identified by a sign to southbound traffic. Please enjoy the view from the road only, since a strip of private land separates Finger Rock from the road.

An alternative route for northbound travelers starts at the intersection <0.0> of Colorado Highways 131 and 134. Proceed north on 131 through the town of Toponas <0.6>, past a side road <6.1> on the left that leads to the Finger Rock State Trout Rearing Unit, to Finger Rock <7.1> on the right (east) side of the road. For northbound motorists, Finger Rock is identified by a sign. If you wish to stop, please pull off the highway completely or pull off onto a side road as no proper parking turnout is provided.

# 7 FINGER ROCK

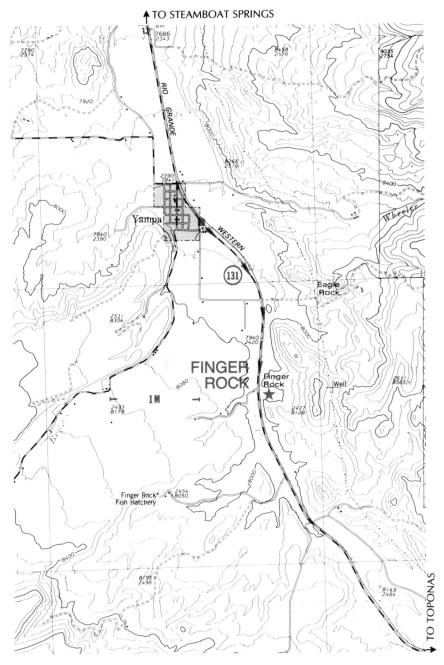

# 8  GORE CANYON

TYPE: Mountain Scenery/Historic
ADMINISTRATION: BLM land/Private land
QUALITY: Very scenic
ACCESS: Good dirt road
FACILITIES: None
TIME NEEDED: Half hour
BEST VISIT: Spring to fall
BEST PHOTO: Afternoon
ELEVATION: 7,752 feet (Inspiration Point)
REFERENCE: Kremmling
MAP: State highway map
Routt National Forest visitor map
USGS TOPO: Kremmling 15' (1956)
USGS COUNTY: Grand County Sheet 3 of 4 (1978)

Inspiration Point is the very fitting name given to a dramatic shelf road overlook blasted from the south wall of Gore Canyon at its western terminus. The view of this four-mile long, 2,000-foot deep canyon is indeed inspirational. The Colorado River, 500 feet below, has cut the steep-walled canyon from the erosion-resistant Precambrian granite of the Gore Range. Gore Canyon is surprisingly colorful for a granite feature. Gentle pastels of orange, red, green, blue, and violet are subtly intermingled among the grays of the igneous bedrock. The canyon is named in honor of Sir St. George Gore, Baronet, who conducted a hunting party of legendary proportions in this area in 1854 (see site 7).

Most of the interesting history about Gore Canyon concerns the tracks of the Denver and Rio Grande Western Railroad on the north wall of the canyon. This line was not always owned by the D & RGW; it was once part of the Moffat Road, known formally as the Denver, Northwestern and Pacific, a railway that was to run from Denver to Salt Lake City. Even before the inception of the Moffat Road, Gore Canyon had been planned as a route for several other railroads, though none began construction in the canyon. While the Moffat Road between Kremmling and Steamboat Springs was being located, David Moffat had to choose between Gore Canyon and Gore Pass as alternative routes for the line. The Gore Canyon option would present considerable construction and maintenance difficulties, but it offered one important strategic advantage. If funds were exhausted before the line was completed, Moffat could extend the Gore Canyon route along the Colorado River to the D & RGW tracks at Dotsero and sell his holdings to that railroad. He decided to build through the canyon, and a claim was filed for this right-of-way.

Things were not to go smoothly, though. In January of 1903, an independent power company announced plans to dam Gore Canyon as part of a power plant project. Moffat considered this a potential scam, as many small companies were hurriedly formed with the intent of extracting exorbitant

# 8 GORE CANYON

The D&RGW Railroad grade is visible just above the Colorado River in this west-end view of Gore Canyon.

# 8 GORE CANYON

right-of-way sums from the railroad. This was a period of serious competition among adversary railroads in the West; thus, this activity could simply be a ploy to halt progress of the line.

The power company began buying up land around Kremmling, paying up to 20 times its true value. To strengthen its claim on the right-of-way, the railroad began construction near the canyon, but someone began to file for reservoirs along other strategic points of the railroad's alignment. Then, the power company blocked work in Gore Canyon when it secured a court injunction against the railroad, but the railroad was successful in overturning this injunction and obtaining another to prevent the power company from using the railroad right-of-way. The power company sold its rights to a different power company, and it was later discovered that the railroad's original filing for right-of-way had been mysteriously lost and never made it to Washington. By this time, it was obvious that a major scandal was in the making.

Without warning, the Department of the Interior announced that it was starting its own reservoir project at Gore Canyon. Apparently someone had suggested this area as an ideal reservoir site for the system being planned by the government to supply California with Colorado River water. The battle increased with more hearings and court cases until the President of the United States took notice. Teddy Roosevelt invited the interested parties to Washington and personally decided the fate of Gore Canyon: the railroad would go through.

With some difficulty, the roadbed was constructed through the canyon. Rockslides continue to be a maintenance problem even today. The line was never completed west of Craig, owing to lack of capital. In 1931, the D & RGW obtained a controlling interest in the line through massive stock purchase. The Dotsero Cutoff was completed shortly thereafter, reducing the D & RGW rail distance between Denver and Salt Lake City by 175 miles.

There are no facilities at Gore Canyon. Care should be taken near the edge of the turnout, as there is no guardrail or fence between you and the bottom of the canyon. Even though the eastern end of the canyon is on private land, it can be viewed from US Highway 40 just north of Kremmling; the western end of the canyon is on BLM property.

**DIRECTIONS:** Proceed south on Colorado 9 from its junction <0.0> with US 40 in Kremmling. Beyond a bridge <1.9> marked by a small sign identifying the Colorado River, there is a junction with a paved road to the right marked by a sign identifying Trough Road (with an arrow), Pump-house Recreation Area (12.5 miles), State Bridge (29 miles), and Wolcott (44 miles). Turn right at this intersection <2.2> and follow this well graveled road that crosses private land for several miles. After passing a small rock window <8.6> on the right, the road becomes good pavement <9.1> and starts to descend toward the canyon. There is a sharp turn

# 8 GORE CANYON

<11.1> to the left protected by a guardrail where the road joins the west end of Gore Canyon. A short distance ahead on the right is a gravel turnout <11.3>. This spot is known as Inspiration Point. This graveled road continues in the Colorado River canyon to its junction with Colorado 131 at State Bridge.

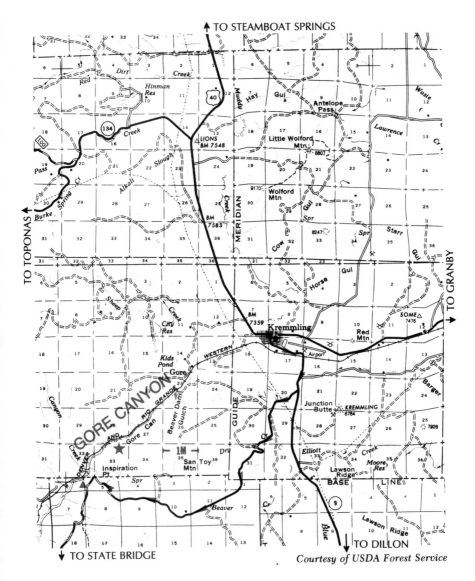

*Courtesy of USDA Forest Service*

# FRONT RANGE DISTRICT

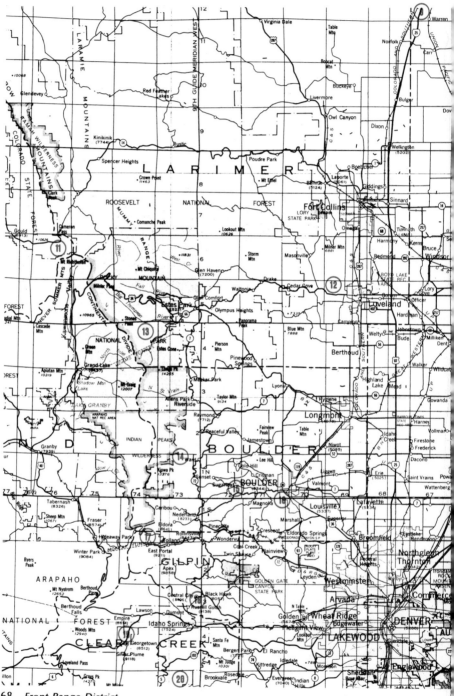

# FRONT RANGE DISTRICT

9 Natural Fort
10 Pawnee Buttes
11 Nokhu Crags
12 Devils Backbone
13 Rocky Mountain National Park
14 Indian Peaks
15 Boulder Falls
16 Royal Arch
17 Moffat Road
18 Central City
19 Georgetown
20 Mount Evans Highway

# 9  NATURAL FORT

TYPE: Plains Scenery/Geologic/Historic
ADMINISTRATION: Public land—Colorado Highway Department
QUALITY: Scenic
ACCESS: Paved road
FACILITIES: None
TIME NEEDED: Half hour
BEST VISIT: All year
BEST PHOTO: All day
ELEVATION: 5,910 feet (base of formation)
REFERENCE: I-25 at Wyoming border
MAP: State highway map
BLM Eaton 1:100,000
USGS TOPO: Carr West 7.5' (1972)
USGS COUNTY: Weld County Sheet 1 of 7 (1978)

Natural Fort is a strong and defendable structure sculpted from sandstone by erosion. Two large outcroppings of white sandstone are accessible from the rest areas on Interstate 25, one east of the highway at the northbound rest area and the other west of the highway at the southbound rest area. Both formations have been heavily weathered, having many depressions, crevices, slots, passageways, potholes, and open spaces within their walls.

The eastern mass is the larger of the two, with walls as tall as 30 feet and longer than 80 feet. There are numerous tight and easily defendable passageways leading to the interior of the fort. Several internal open areas are well protected by the nearly continuous walls, which never dip below 10 feet in height. The western structure is a sandstone-ringed, grassy-bottomed corral with a natural entrance to the north. Several small natural openings, or windows, one to two feet in diameter can be found in the sandstone of the western fort. Other outcroppings of the same white sandstone can be seen to the east, but none looks as interestingly weathered as Natural Fort.

While you drive south from the state line on Interstate 25, you see subtle changes in the vicinity's sedimentary geology. The highway initially crosses a layer of rough and gravelly sandstone deposited during the Tertiary period. The road gradually drops onto a layer of fine-grained white sandstone of the Oligocene White River formation, laid down 26 to 38 million years ago. This is the sandstone that constitutes Natural Fort. The naturally white sandstone has been tinted gray by patchy remains of lichen that once grew on its surface. The still-living splotches of lichen are mostly orange in color. The soft sandstone forming the fort is highly weathered because of the poor quality of the cementing compounds binding the grains of sand together.

East of here, the Tertiary sediments have yielded many fossil remains of large mammals and reptiles. Leaving the Tertiary layers, the highway descends to an older stratum of Upper Cretaceous sandstone of the Mesozoic era near the Carr exit. This sandstone was once beach sand at the edge of the Cretaceous sea. Further south, the highway enters an area of Pierre shale,

# 9   NATURAL FORT

The walls of Natural Fort stand high above this visitor.

Erosion has sculpted this sandstone into intricate designs.

# 9  NATURAL FORT

where land use changes because the shale forms a soil much better suited to farming than the previous layers of sandstone, which are useful only as grazing land.

Natural Fort is named for its history as well as its geology. It was used as a stronghold and place of battle during the nineteenth century and undoubtedly before. There are stories of bandits hiding their loot in the formation's recesses, of travelers taking refuge from belligerent Indians or outlaws, and of ferocious Indian battles continuing until the white breastworks were stained red from the blood of the victims.

The most famous of these confrontations took place between the Blackfoot and Crow tribes. An unrelenting drought in 1831 forced herds of buffalo that normally foraged north of Colorado to follow the dwindling streams and rivers to their sources in the Colorado Rocky Mountains. Indian tribes that hunted buffalo for food in the present Yellowstone National Park region were forced to follow. Hunting bands of Blackfoot and Crow, traditional adversaries, both converged on the Natural Fort area in pursuit of game. A group of about 600 Crow surprised a band of around 160 Blackfoot hunters and pursued them to Natural Fort. The encounter ended with a bloody battle in which the Crow killed all of the Blackfoot tribesmen one at a time. Jim Beckwourth, the mulatto leader of the Crow, admitted to the personal slaughter of only 11 Blackfoot warriors—a modest boast for Jim.

Both the northbound and southbound rest areas have an informative sign on the history of Natural Fort. The rest area's rest rooms have been removed.

**DIRECTIONS:** Because Interstate Highway 25 runs through its middle, this location is easily reached. Natural Fort is adjacent to a pair of rest areas on both the northbound and southbound lanes of I-25. The area is just three miles south of the Wyoming state line between mile-markers 295 and 296.

Northbound traffic on I-25 will enter Weld County (identified by a small sign) just before encountering exit 293 for Carr <0.0>. This is the last exit before the Wyoming border. The northbound rest area is north of this exit and is identified by a sign. Exit at this rest area <3.1> for Natural Fort. When you leave the rest area, no exit is available to return in the southbound direction until you travel a short distance into Wyoming.

Southbound traffic on I-25 in Wyoming will encounter the Colorado state line <0.0> at Colorado mile-marker 299. At the state boundary, there is a large sign welcoming the visitor to Colorado. There is also a small sign identifying this as Weld County. Just south of mile-marker 296 is a rest area <3.0> identified by a sign. Exit here for Natural Fort. If you wish to return to Wyoming after leaving the rest area, you must first continue south three miles to exit 293 for Carr, where you can exit and then reenter I-25 in the northbound direction.

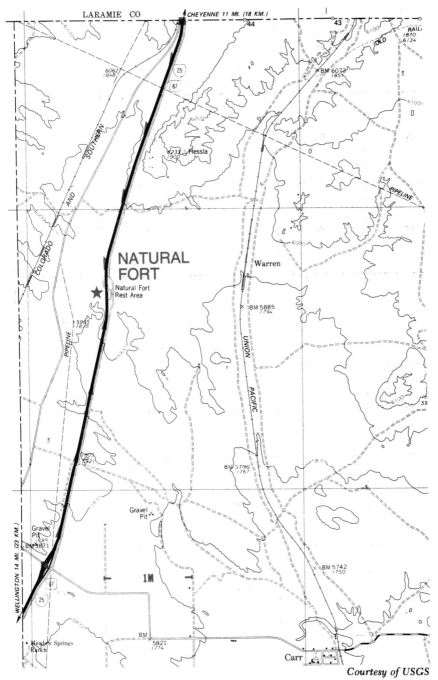

Courtesy of USGS

# 10  PAWNEE BUTTES

TYPE: Plains Scenery/Geologic/Paleontologic
ADMINISTRATION: Pawnee National Grassland/Private land
QUALITY: Scenic
ACCESS: Good dirt road
FACILITIES: None
TIME NEEDED: Half hour to all day
BEST VISIT: Spring or fall
BEST PHOTO: Afternoon to late afternoon
ELEVATION: 5,375 feet (top of east butte)
REFERENCE: Keota
MAP: Pawnee National Grassland visitor map
USGS TOPO: Pawnee Buttes 7.5′ (1977)
USGS COUNTY: Weld County Sheet 2 of 7 (1978)

Pawnee Buttes, in Pawnee National Grassland, are perhaps the most dramatic landforms of the Colorado eastern plains. Standing nearly 250 feet above the surrounding terrain, these twin formations have defied the forces of erosion. The lower portions of the buttes are composed of relatively soft, clay-like sedimentary rock (the Brule formation). These lower components are protected by an upper layer of sandstone and conglomerate sediments (the Arikaree formation) which are more resistant to the wear and tear of the elements. The weathering process has left this pair standing in isolation despite the fact that all the similar surrounding material has worn away.

The Pawnee Buttes area is one of the finest vertebrate fossil collection sites in the world. Skeletons of mammals and other creatures of Miocene and Oligocene times have been preserved here. As early as the 1870s, Yale Professor O. C. Marsh studied fossil remains of now extinct forms of the horse and a giraffe-like camel (*Alticamelus*). The area has yielded fossils of birds, a huge bear-dog creature (*Amphicyon*), a giant rhinoceros-like animal (*Titanothere*) that was once the most abundant form of mammal in the western United States, a large horse-like animal with claws (*Chalicothere*), ancient tapirs, and many other types of ancestral or extinct mammals. Fossils found here contributed significantly toward understanding the evolution of the horse. An excellent display of fossil skeletons characteristic of this area can be found at the Museum of Natural History in Denver.

These buttes once served as landmarks for a tribal meeting place and were part of the Pawnee Indian hunting grounds. This has been grazing land for centuries. Though the great herds of bison are gone, this forage is now heavily used by beef cattle. Wild animals of the area include pronghorn antelope, mule deer, coyote, and a variety of birds including the abundant prairie falcon.

Be sure to fill your fuel tank before visiting this sparsely inhabited region of Colorado. There are no sources of water or any other facilities near the buttes. While walking in the area, watch carefully for cacti and rattlesnakes.

Pawnee Buttes stand in abrupt contrast to the usually level terrain of northeastern Colorado.

Closer examination of the east butte shows a small rock protrusion on its summit.

# 10  PAWNEE BUTTES

**DIRECTIONS:** Proceed east on Colorado 14 from its intersection <0.0> with Interstate 25 toward the town of Ault. Continue east (straight) on Colorado 14 at its intersection <14.1> with US 85 in Ault. Continue past the Pawnee National Grassland boundary <26.9> and beyond the town of Briggsdale <36.9> on the right. Be sure to notice the view <42.9> of the Chalk Cliffs far to the north from along this stretch of Colorado 14. Ignore a dirt road <49.8> to the left (north) marked by a sign identifying this as the turn for Keota. Just 3.8 miles beyond this intersection is a junction <53.6> with a gravel road that runs northwest (left) at a 45-degree angle from Colorado 14. This road is not marked by a sign for eastbound travelers on Highway 14, but for westbound traffic a sign identifies it as the turn for Keota, Hereford, and Grover. Turn left (north-west) at this intersection, and head northwest on this gravel road (Weld County 390). Continue past a side road <58.4> to the left (identified as Road 105 by a small green sign) to the junction <58.8> with a side road to the right (north), labeled as Road 105 by a small green sign. Turn right onto this side road, which passes just east of Keota, a town containing a handful of buildings and a water tower as its most prominent feature. After several curves, this road comes to a T-intersection <62.0> with an east-west road labeled Road 104 by a small green sign. Turn right (east) at this junction and continue exactly three miles to the intersection <65.0> with a side road to the left (north) marked as Road 111. Turn left at this junction and continue north past a side road <68.0> to the right labeled Road 110 by a small green sign. The road curves to the left (west) and encounters an improved dirt road <69.2> to the right (north).

Turn right and follow this good dirt road as it climbs a hill and heads to the east. Continue until the road comes to a parking area <70.3> just left (north) of a windmill. Park in the area provided. There is a good view of the Buttes to the northeast in the shallow valley below. At the southern end of the parking area is a sign that marks the beginning of the Pawnee Buttes Trail. This well beaten path continues from here a little over a mile to the base of the Pawnee Buttes below.

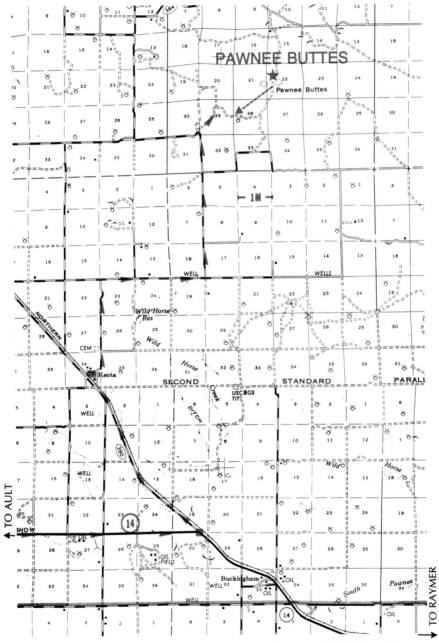

*Courtesy of USDA Forest Service*

# 11  NOKHU CRAGS

TYPE: Mountain Scenery
ADMINISTRATION: Public land—Colorado State Forest
QUALITY: Very scenic
ACCESS: Paved road
FACILITIES: Campgrounds and picnic areas
TIME NEEDED: Half hour
BEST VISIT: Spring to fall
BEST PHOTO: Afternoon
ELEVATION: 12,485 feet (highest crag)
REFERENCE: Teds Place
MAP: State highway map
Roosevelt National Forest visitor map
USGS TOPO: Mount Richthofen 7.5' (1977)
Clark Peak 7.5' (1962)
USGS COUNTY: Jackson County Sheet 4 of 4 (1978)

Nokhu Crags are 0.6 miles north of Static Peak, which is on the Continental Divide. They form the lofty and ragged northern terminus of the Never Summer Range, the western boundary of Rocky Mountain National Park. The view of these rock projections is dramatic from several points along Colorado 14. The crags are within Colorado's only state forest, which encompasses most of the forested western slopes of the Medicine Bow Mountains. The forest offers hiking, camping, and fishing, but a Colorado parks pass is required if you leave the highway.

The drive on Colorado 14 from its junction with US 287 to the Colorado State Forest is in itself a scenic adventure. This route follows the Cache la Poudre River, which got its name (meaning "hide the powder") when wagons belonging to mountain men from the Hudson Bay Fur Company became stuck in the deep snow of November 1836. To lighten the load, they were forced to stash barrels of gunpowder near the banks of the river until the following spring.

**DIRECTIONS:** Proceed north from Fort Collins on US 287 to its junction with Colorado 14 at Teds Place. Turn left (west) at this junction <0.0> and follow paved Colorado 14 all the way to Nokhu Crags. This route will lead you past many campground and picnic areas and many points of interest: a tunnel <14.7>, Profile Rock <34.1> (the likeness of a man's face), Home Range Geologic Site <37.5>, Poudre State Fish Rearing Unit <38.8>, Sleeping Elephant Mountain <43.5> (which resembles its namesake in the late afternoon light), Poudre Falls <47.5>, a Roosevelt National Forest Information Station <50.6>, and Joe Wright Reservoir <55.4>. A paved turnout <57.7> on the right (north) side of the road offers a scenic view of Nokhu Crags. Continue over Cameron Pass <58.1> to a turnout <59.4> on the left (south) side of the highway. This turnout and another <60.0> both offer excellent views of the Crags.

# 11 NOKHU CRAGS

Nokhu Crags stand as sentinels at the northern end of the Never Summer Range.

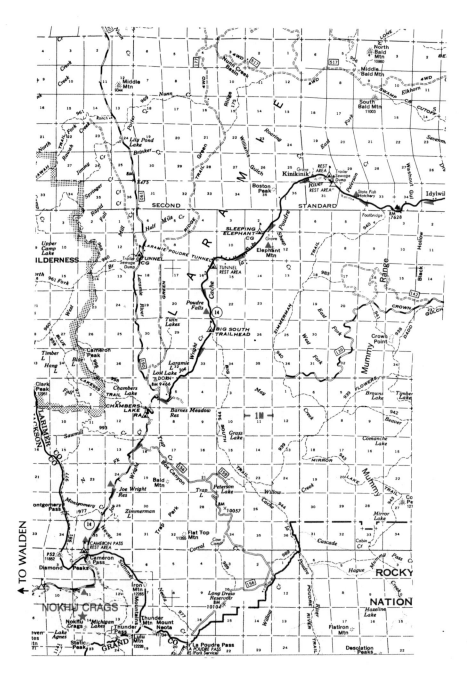

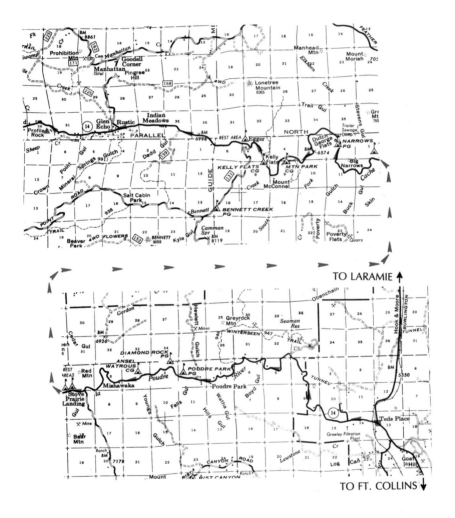

Courtesy of USDA Forest Service

# 12  DEVILS BACKBONE

| | |
|---:|:---|
| **TYPE:** | Foothills Scenery/Geologic |
| **ADMINISTRATION:** | Private land |
| **QUALITY:** | Scenic |
| **ACCESS:** | Paved road |
| **FACILITIES:** | None |
| **TIME NEEDED:** | Quarter hour |
| **BEST VISIT:** | Spring or fall |
| **BEST PHOTO:** | Afternoon to late afternoon |
| **ELEVATION:** | 5,320 feet (Keyhole) |
| **REFERENCE:** | Loveland |
| **MAP:** | State highway map |
| | Roosevelt National Forest visitor map |
| **USGS TOPO:** | Masonville 7.5' (1971) |
| **USGS COUNTY:** | Larimer County Sheet 4 of 4 (1978) |

Devils Backbone is a prominent outcropping just north of US 34 and west of the town of Loveland. The ragged-topped formation contains several small natural openings, or windows, and one large aperture known as the Keyhole. From the road, the Keyhole appears to be small, but it stands over 20 feet tall. It appears small only in comparison to the great size of the Backbone, a vertical mass of rock composed of Dakota Sandstone. Fossilized shells of large sea turtles found in this layer indicate this area was once ocean front property. You may wonder how a layer of rock that started out as beach sand ended up vertical. As the present-day Rocky Mountains rose, the nearby sedimentary layers were tilted and contorted to form hogbacks that typify the transition between the sedimentary plains and the igneous granite mountains. At one time, the Dakota Sandstone curved from the top of the formation to join another Dakota Sandstone hogback to the east, forming a type of dome. Erosion has removed the dome, leaving this vertical wall isolated from its hogback counterpart. Because Devils Backbone is on private property, please enjoy it only from the road.

**DIRECTIONS:** Take exit 257B <0.0> on Interstate 25. This places you on westbound US 34 toward Loveland and Estes Park. Continue west on US 34 past its intersection with northbound US 287 <4.2> (the junction with southbound US 287 is one block west) and through Loveland to the Devils Backbone west of town. The east side of the formation is visible from the highway <7.3> which then crosses its southern end <8.5>. A fairly well hidden one-way road to the right leaves US 34 <8.6>, follows the west wall of the formation for a short distance, and then parallels US 34. Good views of the western side of the formation are available from US 34 <9.0> and from a side road that heads north from its intersection <9.3> with the highway. If you continue west, US 34 will take you through scenic Big Thompson Canyon to Estes Park and Rocky Mountain National Park.

# 12 DEVILS BACKBONE

Devils Backbone is a rugged spine in the level terrain just east of the foothills.

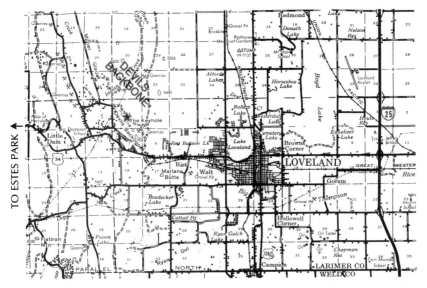

*Courtesy of USDA Forest Service*

# 13 ROCKY MOUNTAIN NATIONAL PARK

**TYPE:** Mountain Scenery
**ADMINISTRATION:** National Park
**QUALITY:** Extremely scenic
**ACCESS:** Paved road
**FACILITIES:** Visitor centers/Campgrounds/Picnic areas
**TIME NEEDED:** One day
**BEST VISIT:** Early summer to fall
**BEST PHOTO:** All day
**ELEVATION:** 12,183 feet (high point on Trail Ridge Road)
**REFERENCE:** Estes Park
**MAP:** State highway map
Roosevelt National Forest visitor map
**USGS TOPO:** Rocky Mountain National Park (1961) 1:62,500
**USGS COUNTY:** Larimer County Sheet 3 of 4 (1977)
Grand County Sheet 2 of 4 (1978)
Boulder County (1980)
Larimer County Sheet 4 of 4 (1978)

Rocky Mountain National Park was established by an act of Congress on January 26, 1915. Its 417 square miles embrace scenery exemplifying Colorado's spectacular mountain geography. The Continental Divide forms the spine of the park, which contains 80 peaks over 10,000 feet and 18 over 12,000 feet. The eastern portions of the park are dominated by Longs Peak (14,255 feet). The east face of this granite hulk is a sheer 2,000-foot diamond-shaped challenge for even the most competent technical mountain climber. The remote mountains of the Mummy Range fill the northern regions of the park and are accessible only by a network of foot trails.

Most of the spectacular mountain scenery of the park was created by glaciers. After the Rocky Mountains rose to their present elevation about five to seven million years ago, a period of severe erosion carved deep V-shaped valleys into the rugged terrain. Then several periods of glaciation gouged rock from the walls of the valleys, leaving them U-shaped, and sliced off large chunks of granite, leaving many of the sheer faces and sharp-edged features characteristic of the park today. You can still see remnants of these glaciers just below the rim of the Continental Divide in the eastern regions of the park.

There are over 300 miles of hiking trails within the park. For those who prefer not to climb the east face of Longs Peak, a 16-mile round-trip hike from Longs Peak trailhead is an alternative route to the summit. This popular trail is a healthy hike with an elevation gain of over 4,000 feet. A certain amount of scrambling is required, and snow and ice on the trail in early summer can be a hazard. Most of the park trails are less demanding than the Longs Peak trail. There are many short walks that lead the visitor to scenic vistas, mountain lakes, fields of wildflowers, and locations for spotting park wildlife. The larger animals include elk (wapiti), mule deer, and the

# 13 ROCKY MOUNTAIN NATIONAL PARK

Flat-topped Longs Peak, a lofty 14,256 feet above sea level, stands behind scenic Bear Lake.

Well into summer, snow covers parts of the hiking trail to Chasm Lake below the east face of Longs Peak.

# 13 ROCKY MOUNTAIN NATIONAL PARK

aloof Rocky Mountain bighorn. Valley meadows near the forest's edge often attract elk and deer, but the bighorn prefer the isolation of the higher altitudes in remote areas of the park. A natural mineral lick in Horseshoe Park near Sheep Lake sometimes coaxes the bighorn into the open. Smaller animals include the marmot (which resembles a woodchuck), pikas that live in rocky areas of the tundra, elusive coyote, beaver, many species of birds, and the ever-present chipmunk and golden-mantled ground squirrel. Please do not approach any of the animals too closely.

Trail Ridge Road (US 34), the highest continuous paved road in the United States, crosses the park. Unlike most mountain highways, which stay in the valleys whenever possible, this road generally follows an old Ute Indian trail over the ridge tops. More than 11 miles, offering spectacular views, cross above timberline. Trail Ridge Road is closed by winter snows, but the Park Service tries to open it by Memorial Day weekend—if the weather cooperates, of course. Before Trail Ridge Road was built, Fall River Road was used to cross the park. This graveled road, which runs parallel to the eastern part of Trail Ridge Road, is open only a short season during mid- to late summer when it is free of snow. It may also be blocked by rockslides. Be sure to take the paved road to Bear Lake, a very scenic portion of the park. Some of the most interesting trails in the park leave from this area.

Facilities in the park include campgrounds (usually full), picnic areas, scenic pullouts, nature trails, and several visitor centers. Each of these visitor centers can provide lots of additional information about the park and its activities. A fee is required to visit the park.

**DIRECTIONS:** From Loveland, take US 34 west to Estes Park through scenic Big Thompson Canyon. On July 31, 1976, heavy rains caused an unprecedented flash flood in this canyon, killing at least 139 people. In Estes Park, at the intersection <0.0> of US 34 and US 36 at a stoplight, there is a large green sign indicating Rocky Mountain National Park access via either Business US 34 and US 36 or Bypass US 34. Take the business route and continue straight toward downtown. A sign marks a left turn for the Administration Building at an intersection <0.4> in town. Turn left at this junction and follow US 36 and the signs that lead you to the park entrance. Continue past the large brown entrance sign <2.5> to the Visitor Center and Park Headquarters <2.9> on the left (south) side of the road. Here, or at the entrance station just beyond, you can get an information brochure containing a map of the park.

An alternative entrance is located at the park's southwestern boundary. An entrance station and Visitor Center are just north of Grand Lake on US 34.

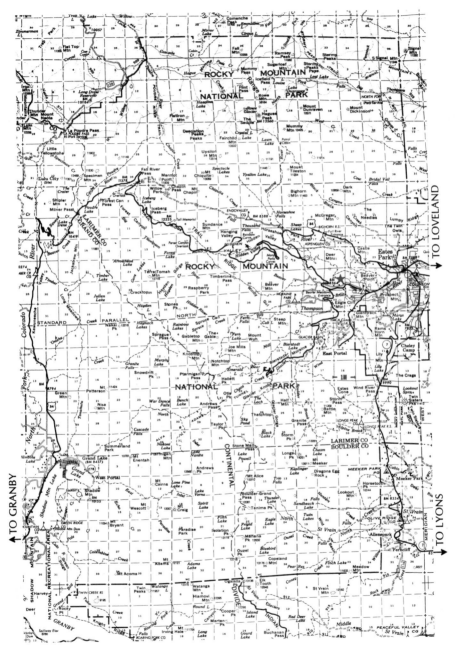

*Courtesy of USDA Forest Service*

# 14   INDIAN PEAKS

TYPE: Mountain Scenery
ADMINISTRATION: Roosevelt National Forest
QUALITY: Very scenic
ACCESS: Paved road
FACILITIES: Campground/Picnic areas
TIME NEEDED: One hour
BEST VISIT: Early summer to fall
BEST PHOTO: Morning
ELEVATION: 10,345 feet (Brainard Lake)
REFERENCE: Ward
MAP: State highway map
Roosevelt National Forest visitor map
USGS TOPO: Ward 7.5' (1978)
USGS COUNTY: Boulder County (1980)

Indian Peaks form the Continental Divide immediately south of Rocky Mountain Park. The collective name "Indian Peaks" refers to the individual peak names: Ogalalla, Paiute, Kiowa, Pawnee, Shoshoni, Apache, Navajo, Arikaree, Arapaho, and others named for Indian tribes of the West. A few peaks, such as Mount Audubon (13,223 feet), offer spectacular views of the area but do not carry the names of tribes. To complement these rugged mountains, there are many scenic lakes nestled along their eastern slopes. A close view of Isabelle Glacier, just above Lake Isabelle, can be reached by trail from the Brainard Lake area. Pawnee Pass (12,541 feet), Buchanan Pass (11,704 feet) to the north, and Arapaho Pass (11,905 feet) to the south are all good places to view the surrounding terrain. Each has trails continuing down the western slopes of the Continental Divide to Monarch Lake. Once a wagon road, Buchanan Pass was named for President James Buchanan, who signed a congressional bill establishing the Colorado Territory in 1861. Later, it was surveyed as a possible railroad route across the Divide. Arapaho Pass was also a lightly used wagon road.

The Brainard Lake Recreation Area of Roosevelt National Forest is a good place to view the Indian Peaks and is easily reached by a paved road from Ward. This recreation area contains a sign (located just east of Brainard Lake) about the Indian Peaks, a campground, numerous picnic facilities, two large parking areas for the trailheads, and a one-way loop road around Brainard Lake. About 55,000 acres, including the Indian Peaks immediately north, west, and south of the recreation area, were closed to development and vehicular traffic in 1965. Congress guaranteed preservation of this untamed area along the Continental Divide, in both Roosevelt and Arapaho national forests, when Indian Peaks Wilderness was established in 1978. Peaks, passes, and high alpine lakes from Rocky Mountain National Park all the way south to Rollins Pass are accessible only by a network of trails. The northern parking area is the trailhead to South St. Vrain Creek, Beaver Creek, Coney Creek, Mount Audubon, Buchanan Pass, Blue Lake, and

A sign names the individual Indian Peaks that stand behind Brainard Lake.

The boulders and gravel in the foreground of this view were deposited long ago by glaciers as they descended from the Continental Divide seen in the background.

# 14 INDIAN PEAKS

Mitchell Lake. The southern parking area has trails leading to Long Lake, Isabelle Glacier, Lake Isabelle, and Pawnee Pass.

Most of the dramatic mountain scenery of the Indian Peaks is due to extensive glaciation about 100,000 years ago. Glaciers were responsible for gouging out basins now occupied by the many lakes of the area. The gravel and boulders between Brainard Lake and the informative sign to its east were piled up by a glacier. Snow fields along the eastern slopes of the peaks, reminders of this last ice age, chill the winds as they roll off the Divide toward Brainard Lake. This has caused a false timberline environment of alpine plants and stunted trees usually not found until you gain an additional 1,200 feet. The melt from this snowpack, an important source of water for inhabitants of eastern Colorado, forms creeks and rivers that have cut several impressive canyons on their journey to the plains.

The Brainard Lake area is quite colorful in the fall when the aspens change. Red Rock Lake, on the south side of the entrance road, is also worthy of a photo stop. In addition, the entrance road offers several good views of early mining activity around Ward. Columbia City, as it was then called, saw its first settlers in 1860. It was later renamed in honor of Calvin Ward, who discovered the area's first profitable mine. Several other successful mines produced gold and, to a lesser degree, other marketable minerals. The narrow-gauge Colorado and Northwestern Railroad, also known as the "Switzerland Trail," transported residents to the town beginning in 1898. Despite the fire of 1910, which destroyed 53 buildings, much of Ward remains occupied.

**DIRECTIONS:** You can reach Brainard Lake by a paved road heading west from Colorado 72 just north of Ward. This intersection is 9.9 miles south of the junction of Colorado Highways 72 and 7 and 11.8 miles north of the junction of Colorado Highways 72 and 119 in Nederland. The turn for this road is marked by a sign identifying Roosevelt National Forest Recreation Area—Brainard Lake. Turn at this intersection <0.0> and follow the paved road west. Where the road begins to climb, you can see Ward and the surrounding mining remains. Continue past a side dirt road <2.6> on the left that goes to Lefthand Reservoir (2 miles). There is a turnout <3.1> on the left (south) side of the road for picturesque Red Rock Lake. Turn right to begin a one-way loop road <4.8> around Brainard Lake. Just to the left (west) after this turn is a turnout with an information sign about the Indian Peaks. The loop road continues past Pawnee Campground, crosses the Brainard Lake outlet, passes several picnic facilities, and comes to an intersection <5.2> with a side road to the right (west). This side road leads to two large parking areas for various trails into the Indian Peaks Wildnerness. The loop road continues around Brainard Lake to rejoin the two-way road <5.8> back to Ward. This area is very popular and often crowded.

# 14  INDIAN PEAKS

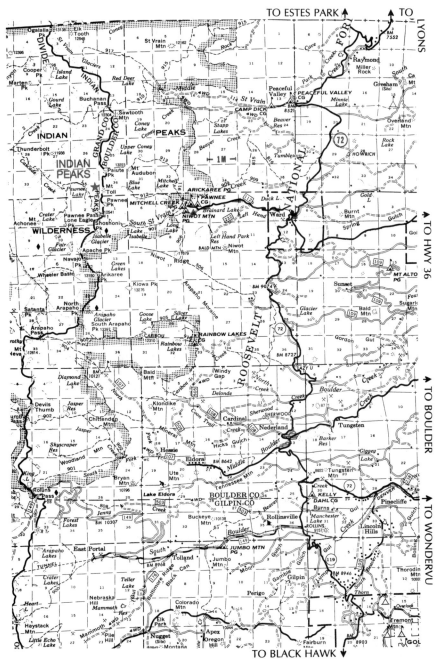

TO ESTES PARK

TO LYONS

TO HWY 36

TO BOULDER

TO WONDERVU

TO BLACK HAWK

*Courtesy of USDA Forest Service*

# 15  BOULDER FALLS

TYPE: Mountain Scenery
ADMINISTRATION: Public land—Boulder County Park
QUALITY: Scenic
ACCESS: Paved road
FACILITIES: None
TIME NEEDED: Half hour
BEST VISIT: July
BEST PHOTO: Early afternoon
ELEVATION: 7,060 feet (base of falls)
REFERENCE: Boulder
MAP: State highway map
Roosevelt National Forest visitor map
USGS TOPO: Gold Hill 7.5' (1978)
USGS COUNTY: Boulder County (1980)

Boulder Falls is a picturesque cascade on the North Fork of Boulder Creek, just two-tenths of a mile before it joins the Middle Fork of Boulder Creek in the main Boulder Canyon. These falls are in a small park administered by Boulder County; the park closes at dark. On the north side of the highway in Boulder Canyon, there is a sign identifying the falls, along with a small display showing a map of the area. Nearby, a rock is displayed that exhibits some interesting results of water erosion. A somewhat improved trail has been constructed on the west side of North Boulder Creek along the short path from the road to the falls. There are no facilities at the falls park, but several picnic areas are on Forest Service land within Boulder Canyon.

The canyons of this region were formed by stream erosion during late Pliocene times, when the present-day Front Range was uplifted. The falls are a result of an unequal rise in the granite during this uplift. This has caused North Boulder Creek to occupy a hanging canyon, a vertical break in the granite, from which it must drop to join with the Middle Boulder Creek. On your drive, watch for technical rock climbers who practice on the canyon walls.

**DIRECTIONS:** From the junction <0.0> of Colorado Highways 119 and 93 (Canyon Boulevard and Broadway respectively) in downtown Boulder, proceed west on Highway 119 toward the mountains. This paved road follows the Middle Fork of Boulder Creek through Boulder Canyon to Nederland. Continue west through the tunnel <4.0>, past the Roosevelt National Forest sign <5.3> to a parking area <8.6> on the left (south) side of the road. Park here, cross the road, and walk to the west side of the creek that goes under the highway. Follow the improved trail (sometimes slippery) about two-tenths of a mile to the falls.

An alternative route begins in Nederland at the junction <0.0> of Colorado Highways 119 and 72. Follow 119 east past Barker Reservoir and Dam <1.6> toward Boulder. Continue past several picnic areas and scenic narrows to the Boulder Falls parking area <7.5> on the right.

# 15  BOULDER FALLS

Boulder Falls is a fine example of Colorado's many scenic cascades.

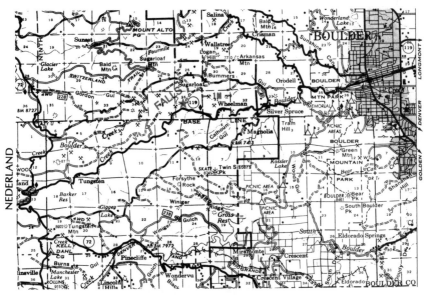

*Courtesy of USDA Forest Service*

# 16 ROYAL ARCH

TYPE: Foothills Scenery/Geologic
ADMINISTRATION: Public land—Boulder Mountain Park
QUALITY: Scenic
ACCESS: Paved road and hike
FACILITIES: Nearby picnic areas
TIME NEEDED: Half day
BEST VISIT: Spring to fall
BEST PHOTO: Morning
ELEVATION: 6,840 feet (arch)
REFERENCE: Boulder
MAP: Roosevelt National Forest visitor map
USGS TOPO: Eldorado Springs 7.5' (1975)
USGS COUNTY: Boulder County (1980)

Boulder is nestled against the foothills of the Rocky Mountain Front Range where Boulder Creek forms a long canyon opening upon the plains of eastern Colorado. The southwestern boundary of town is a series of up-turned sedimentary rock slabs known as the Flatirons. Contained within one of the town's mountain parks, the Flatirons are part of a layer that once lay horizontal. They were formed from sediments resulting from erosion of the Ancestral Rockies, an early formation created 300 million years ago. The erosion of these mountains provided the building material for many of the sedimentary layers that are now the horizontal surface strata of the eastern plains. Some of this eroded material formed gently sloping fan-shaped masses of gravel and sand (alluvial fans) where a mountain stream emptied into the level plain. As the Ancestral Rockies were completely eroded, additional material was deposited atop these fans. Over millions of years, the weight helped to convert the fans into sandstone and conglomerate. As the present Rockies were uplifted, between 50 and 70 million years ago, the granite that arose fractured and tilted these layers where the mountains met the plains. The resulting slabs that rest against the foothills in a steeply tilted fashion are the Flatirons. In this formation, a 20-foot natural arch resulted from faulting and frost erosion.

The arch is accessible by a foot trail slightly over two miles long (one way). The occasionally steep trail gains 1,200 feet on its way to the top of the Flatirons, where the arch is situated, and passes just below the third Flati-ron, where you often can watch technical climbing teams at work. The trail also offers several sweeping views of Boulder and the plains to the east. You may wish to carry water on this hike.

The end of the trail near the arch also provides good views of the town to the northeast and of the National Center for Atmospheric Research to the southeast. To photograph the arch, walk through its opening to the south side and out onto a sandstone rock that extends only a few feet beyond the arch. Be careful of the sheer drop from this point. A wide-angle lens is helpful in photographing the arch, which is best illuminated in the late

# 16  ROYAL ARCH

The top of one of the Flatirons can be seen through the opening of Royal Arch.

# 16   ROYAL ARCH

morning sunlight. The metal guard around the trunk of the large pine tree at the base of the arch is to protect it from wear and tear by many visitors that take this popular hike.

**DIRECTIONS:** From the junction <0.0> of Colorado Highways 119 and 93 (Canyon Boulevard and Broadway respectively) in downtown Boulder, proceed south on 93 (Broadway) to Baseline Road <1.4>. Turn right at this junction and proceed west to just past 9th Street. Turn left (south) into Chautauqua Park <2.4> directly across from Grant Street. Almost immediately after making this turn you must turn left into a parking area. Park here, and you may wish to consult the displayed map of the park for orientation and information about other park activities and hiking trails. The trail to Royal Arch is included in this display.

Follow the path as it leads up the hill along Bluebell Canyon toward the Bluebell Shelter. The shelter is a little over a half-mile walk. The trail to Royal Arch leaves the path from its southernmost point on a curve just south and down the hill from the shelter. The trailhead is marked by a sign. There are occasionally other markers along the trail to help the hiker navigate the proper course.

The trail begins by dropping a little and then parallels Bluebell Canyon, staying on its northwest side for a distance. After you cross through a wooded area, you can see the third Flatiron towering above the trail just to the west. The trail crosses to the southeastern side of Bluebell Canyon and then starts to climb steeply via a series of switchbacks. The trail gains elevation as it heads toward the top of the Flatirons. Here, the drainage for Bluebell Canyon has cut a gap in the sedimentary formation that makes the Flatirons. This section of the trail is through a heavily forested area, but it offers a view of the southeast across Boulder where it tops out near a sedimentary rock outcropping. The trail then drops 80 feet as it traverses the next drainage to the south and rises over more switchbacks as it approaches the top of another rock outcropping. The arch is in this formation but is hidden from view by trees until you are just under it.

After you return from Royal Arch, you may wish to continue west on Baseline Road where you enter more of the Boulder Mountain Park and ascend Flagstaff Mountain via a series of switchbacks on a paved road. From the top of the mountain, you can see east over the town of Boulder as well as west across Boulder Canyon toward the Continental Divide.

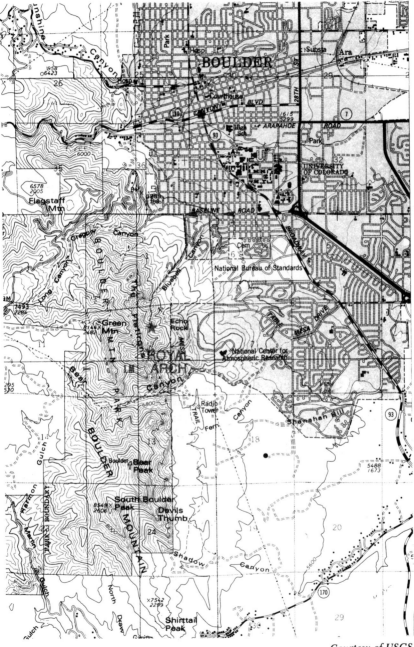

*Courtesy of USGS*

# 17  MOFFAT ROAD

TYPE: Mountain Scenery/Historic
ADMINISTRATION: Roosevelt, Arapaho National Forests/Private land
QUALITY: Very scenic
ACCESS: Rough dirt road
FACILITIES: Picnic ground along east access
TIME NEEDED: Half day
BEST VISIT: Midsummer to late summer
BEST PHOTO: All day
ELEVATION: 11,671 feet (Rollins Pass)
REFERENCE: Rollinsville
MAP: State highway map
Roosevelt National Forest visitor map
Arapaho National Forest visitor map
USGS TOPO: Nederland 7.5' (1972)
East Portal 7.5' (1958)
Fraser 7.5' (1957)
USGS COUNTY: Gilpin County (1980)
Boulder County (1980)
Grand County Sheet 4 of 4 (1978)

Denver banker David H. Moffat incorporated the Denver, Northwestern and Pacific Railway Company on July 18, 1902. The railroad, better known as the Moffat Road, was to run from Denver to Salt Lake and cross the Continental Divide near Denver, where the rough terrain provided the shortest possible route between the terminal cities. To avoid the problems of a climbing route in this rugged stretch of mountains, plans included a tunnel under the Continental Divide. A temporary route built over the Divide until the tunnel could be completed became the most challenging and scenic portion of the Moffat Road. Though intended for only three or four years' use, this route served as the main line for 24 years until the completion of the Moffat Tunnel in 1927.

The "Hill" route follows the valley of South Boulder Creek to the beginning of the long climb toward the Continental Divide. As the road ascends, it offers many fine views of the surrounding mountain scenery from the numerous curves and switchbacks. At one point, the road almost encircles Yankee Doodle Lake—the most heavily advertised scenic spot on the route. At the end of a long, straight stretch of track, the route passes through a short tunnel called the Needle's Eye, then turns and crosses the twin trestles clinging to the mountainside across the Devil's Slide, high above the valley of Middle Boulder Creek. Next is the summit, Rollins Pass, a spectacular place to view the Continental Divide. The line then descends and, at one point, makes a loop at Rifle Sight Notch with a trestle over a tunnel. The road continues to a point near the present west portal of the Moffat Tunnel.

Recently, the Moffat Road has been maintained as a vehicle route of both scenic and historic value. Unfortunately, the Needle's Eye Tunnel suffered

This trestle over Devil's Slide spans a slope descending over 1,000 feet to the valley floor below. The trestles are now closed to vehicles.

# 17  MOFFAT ROAD

major rock falls in the spring of 1979 and again in 1982, but has since been reinforced. In addition, the Devil's Slide trestles have been determined unsafe for cars. For this reason, the Forest Service and Boulder County have officially closed the trestles. A four wheel drive road now bypasses the trestles. Thirty five miles of the roadbed can still be driven if you approach from both the east and west, but because the route is no longer maintained as a through road, the Forest Service doesn't recommend it for passenger car travel. The road is rough in places, subject to mud just west of Rollins Pass, and affords few opportunities to turn around. There are no present plans to reopen the route as a through road.

If you have a passenger car, it is worth the trip to visit the east portal of the Moffat Tunnel from Rollinsville over an all-weather, though sometimes rippled, dirt road. The tunnel was constructed between 1923 and 1927 at a cost of 18 million dollars and 19 lives. The 6.21-mile tunnel is the third-longest railroad tunnel in the United States and is over a half-mile deep where it crosses under the Continental Divide. The completion of this tunnel made 23 miles of the "Hill" route over Rollins Pass obsolete and reduced the travel time for a train by nearly 2.5 hours. The Moffat Tunnel now serves as part of the main line of the Denver and Rio Grande Western Railroad and continues to receive a great deal of use.

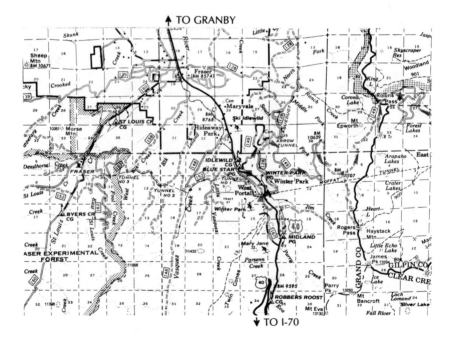

# 17  MOFFAT ROAD

**DIRECTIONS:** Rollinsville is located on Colorado Highway 119, just 4.8 miles south of its junction with Colorado 72 in Nederland and 13.6 miles north of its junction with Colorado 279 in Black Hawk. Slightly north of the railroad tracks in Rollinsville, a good dirt road (marked by a sign indicating a turn for Tolland and East Portal) leaves Colorado 119 toward the west. Follow this road from its junction <0.0> with 119 and bear left where a road <0.9> marked by a sign indicating a Ranger Station leaves to the right. Continue past a picnic area <2.6> that offers a schematic map of the Moffat Road. Bear right where a road <5.2> marked by a sign indicating a turn for the townsite of Apex leaves to the left in Tolland. From a T-intersection <7.5> you can turn left to visit the east portal of the Moffat Tunnel or right to begin the Moffat Road (no longer recommended for passenger cars) toward Rollins Pass. You may drive only as far as the Devil's Slide trestles where the road is now closed.

The western approach is from US 40 near Winter Park, just 12.1 miles north of Berthoud Pass or 0.9 miles north of the Moffat Tunnel overlook where US 40 crosses just above the west portal of the tunnel. Turn right on this good dirt road (Forest Road 149) and stay on what appears to be the main road; ignore the numerous side roads. The quality of this road deteriorates as you approach Rollins Pass, and it is no longer recommended for passenger cars. The route can be followed as far as the Devil's Slide trestles, where the road is closed just on the east side of the pass.

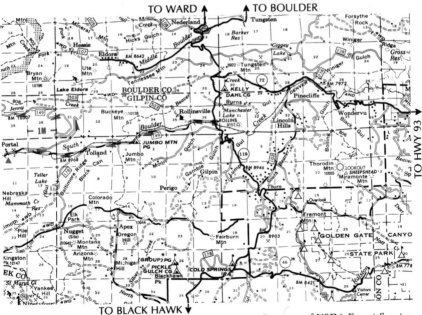

*Courtesy of USDA Forest Service*

# 18 CENTRAL CITY

TYPE: Mountain Scenery/Historic
ADMINISTRATION: Private land
QUALITY: Scenic
ACCESS: Paved road
FACILITIES: Commercial attractions
TIME NEEDED: Half day
BEST VISIT: Spring to fall
BEST PHOTO: Morning to midday
ELEVATION: 8,496 feet
REFERENCE: Central City
MAP: State highway map
Arapaho National Forest visitor map
USGS TOPO: Central City 7.5' (1972)
USGS COUNTY: Gilpin County (1980)

Gregory Gulch, which forms the drainage between Central City and Black Hawk, was the site of one of the first major gold strikes in the state. The Colorado gold rush resulted from the diggings of John H. Gregory of Georgia, who discovered gold here on May 6, 1859. This find led to the mining development of the Central City mineral belt, an area four miles long and two and a half miles wide. This district has produced over 85 million dollars in gold.

To provide a high-class hotel for visitors to the wealthy mining district, the Teller House (open for commercial tours) was built at a cost of over $100,000 in 1872. A point of interest in the Teller House Bar is the "Face on the Bar Room Floor," inspired by a poem of the same name composed by H. Antoine D'Arcy. Another famous structure, the Central City Opera House (also open for commercial tours), was completed in 1878. During the mining boom, it attracted cultural entertainment from all over the world.

Though the population of Central City once exceeded 10,000, the decline of the mining industry left the town virtually deserted by the turn of the century. A cultural renaissance began in 1932 when Lillian Gish starred in a performance of *Camille* in the newly renovated Opera House. The town is now host to many annual cultural activies held at the Opera House. The present town has been restored with many of the historical buildings renovated as commercial attractions and retail shops. Several publications are available giving in-depth accounts of Central City's history.

**DIRECTIONS:** Follow Colorado 279 west from its junction <0.0> with Colorado 119 in Black Hawk. Continue past the Gregory Monument <0.4> to an intersection <1.1> in the center of Central City. Turn left at this intersection to reach the parking lots at the southern edge of town, or continue straight (leaving town) to visit the interesting cemeteries of Central City.

One of Colorado's most famous mining towns, Central City, is located in the "richest square mile on earth."

*Courtesy of USDA Forest Service*

# 19 GEORGETOWN

| | |
|---|---|
| **TYPE:** | Mountain Scenery/Historic |
| **ADMINISTRATION:** | Private land |
| **QUALITY:** | Scenic |
| **ACCESS:** | Paved road |
| **FACILITIES:** | Commercial attractions |
| **TIME NEEDED:** | Half day |
| **BEST VISIT:** | Spring to fall |
| **BEST PHOTO:** | Midday |
| **ELEVATION:** | 8,519 feet |
| **REFERENCE:** | Georgetown |
| **MAP:** | State highway map |
| | Arapaho National Forest visitor map |
| **USGS TOPO:** | Georgetown 7.5' (1974) |
| **USGS COUNTY:** | Clear Creek County (1980) |

The discovery of gold in Clear Creek valley led to the birth of Georgetown in 1859. Placer (surface) mining provided a boom for the area until the claims began to give out, but a second rush began in the 1870s with the development of hard rock mining. Before Leadville boomed in 1878, Georgetown was the principal silver producer in the state. High ore prices caused a few mines to reopen in 1933, but little mining activity exists in the vicinity today.

A narrow-gauge railroad reached Georgetown in 1877, but extension of the line up the valley to Silver Plume presented a difficult problem. The elevation gain was over 600 feet in the two-mile distance to Silver Plume, resulting in a grade of 6 percent—too steep for a locomotive. This problem was solved by the construction of the Georgetown Loop. Tracks were laid up the valley, gaining elevation on the valley wall, to a hairpin turn. From there, the tracks headed back toward Georgetown. Another hairpin curve, this time a high metal trestle, turned the line back toward Silver Plume, crossing over Clear Creek and the tracks below. The loop lengthened the distance between the two cities but held the grade to 3 percent. It became a major tourist attraction in its day and has been partially restored (commercial train trips are available).

Perhaps the most famous structure in town is the Hotel de Paris. During the 1880s and '90s, it was one of the best known and most glorious hotels west of the Mississippi. Louis Du Puy, injured by a mining accident, purchased a bakery in town and had converted it into a hotel by 1875. This establishment was luxurious and elegant, offered exotic cuisine, and soon was the hub of Georgetown society. Today, the hotel and many other structures of unique Victorian architecture have been restored. Some are available for commercial tours. There are several publications available, on Georgetown's history.

**DIRECTIONS:** A large green sign on Interstate 70 proclaims this area as part of the Georgetown Loop National Historical District. Take exit 228 on I-70 for Georgetown. Follow the signs to the historic center of town.

# 19  GEORGETOWN

The Guanella Pass Road offers a good view across Georgetown.

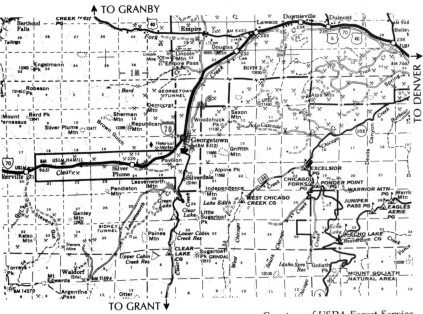

*Courtesy of USDA Forest Service*

# 20 MOUNT EVANS HIGHWAY

**TYPE:** Mountain Scenery
**ADMINISTRATION:** Arapaho National Forest/Denver Mountain Park
**QUALITY:** Very scenic
**ACCESS:** Paved road
**FACILITIES:** Picnic grounds/Campground at Echo Lake
**TIME NEEDED:** Half day
**BEST VISIT:** Midsummer to late summer
**BEST PHOTO:** All day
**ELEVATION:** 14,264 feet (Mount Evans summit)
**REFERENCE:** Idaho Springs
**MAP:** State highway map
Arapahoe National Forest visitor map
**USGS TOPO:** Mount Evans 7.5' (1974)
Harris Peak 7.5' (1974)
Idaho Springs 7.5' (1974)
**USGS COUNTY:** Clear Creek County (1980)

Mount Evans Highway is the highest passenger car road in the world. The road climbs to just below the summit of Mount Evans, the 13th highest peak in Colorado at an altitude of 14,264 feet. This peak was originally named Mount Rosalie by artist Albert Bierstadt in honor of his wife and appears in his famous painting *Storm in the Rocky Mountains*. He completed his first ascent of the mountain in 1863. In 1870, the peak was renamed Mount Evans in honor of Colorado's second territorial governor, John Evans. The first road up the mountain was constructed in the early 1930s but was barely passable until an improved road was completed in 1939.

The highway begins climbing toward the summit in dense forest at Echo Lake. After 3 miles, the road approaches timberline and the northern end of the Mount Goliath Trail. The other end of this trail (Forest Trail 50) rejoins the road 1.8 miles farther ahead (south), where the trailhead is better marked. This trail cuts across the Mount Goliath Natural Area, just east of Goliath Peak (12,216 feet). The 1.1-mile trail traverses subalpine and alpine environments and is a good place to see several bristlecone pines. Many of these pines are more than a thousand years old and are among the oldest living organisms on this planet. The trail's higher elevations offer a variety of alpine plant life, including flowers that bloom in profusion during the short summer season (July and August). The upper trailhead is also the start of a half-mile hike known as the Alpine Garden Loop (Forest Trail 49). In addition to these relatively short trails, the Mount Evans area offers many good hiking opportunities.

The highway continues climbing toward the summit but is now above timberline. Views are in all directions from the road. The occasionally steep drop-off west of the road adds a sense of excitement to this trip. There are several turnouts along the route that offer fine vistas and photographic opportunities. At 8.7 miles from the junction with Colorado 103 is the

Summit Lake is positioned high above timberline with the crest of Mount Evans in the background.

Echo Lake, typical of many of Colorado's mountain lakes, is located just west of the start of the Mount Evans Highway.

# 20 MOUNT EVANS HIGHWAY

parking area for Summit Lake Park, one of the Denver Mountain Parks. Summit Lake is a large, snow-fed body of water nestled in a glacial cirque directly below the summit of Mount Evans. The park offers picnic tables, rest rooms, and a short walk to an impressive viewpoint of the Chicago Lakes, over 2,000 feet below.

The road continues toward the summit via a series of tight switchbacks. Near the top is the Denver Cosmic Ray Research Laboratory. This scientific investigation station was built in 1936 to take advantage of Mount Evans's altitude and proximity to Denver. The thin air at this altitude, which is necessary for minimal interaction between cosmic rays and the atmosphere, provides an excellent cosmic ray study environment. The research structures have been designed to withstand winds over 150 miles per hour. Experiments have been conducted here by Carl Anderson, R. A. Millikan, and A. H. Compton, three American Nobel laureates in physics. Studies have also been made in meteorology and biochemistry.

The road ends in a large parking area just below the summit. Nearby are the burned-out ruins of the Crest House. This 40-year-old structure, where refreshments and souvenirs were sold, was destroyed by fire on Labor Day weekend in 1979. A short walk leads to the summit of Mount Evans. The views are spectacular and encompass a huge area of the state. Fifty miles to the north is Longs Peak, 58 miles to the south is Pikes Peak, and many of Colorado's other "fourteeners" are visible to the west. The weather at the top is often windy and cool, even in the middle of summer, so be sure to bring proper clothing for protection. Also, be sure to return to your vehicle should a lightning storm approach.

**DIRECTIONS:** Take exit 240 <0.0> on Interstate 70, which is identified by a green sign as the exit for Mount Evans and Colorado Highway 103. Proceed south on Colorado 103. You may wish to stop at the Arapaho National Forest Information Station, which is immediately south and west of the Interstate exit off Colorado 103. The station sells copies of all the Colorado National Forest visitor maps and has displays and other sources of information about Arapaho National Forest. Continue on Colorado 103 past the Chicago Forks Picnic Ground <8.1>, past the Ponder Point Picnic Ground <9.9>, and past Echo Lake Park <12.7>. Echo Lake Park, one of Denver's Mountain Parks, has Mount Evans as its backdrop. Echo Lake Campground and Echo Lake Lodge (which offers meals and other facilities) are located at the junction of Colorado Highways 103 and 5. This intersection is marked by a sign that identifies the Mount Evans Highway, the world's highest auto road (14,264 feet). Turn right (south) at this junction <13.2> onto Colorado 5 to begin the 14-mile Mount Evans Highway. Though this road is paved, severe weather conditions, typical of high altitude, often cause potholes and other hazards. The road is not wide, and a few tight turns make it inappropriate for wide vehicles.

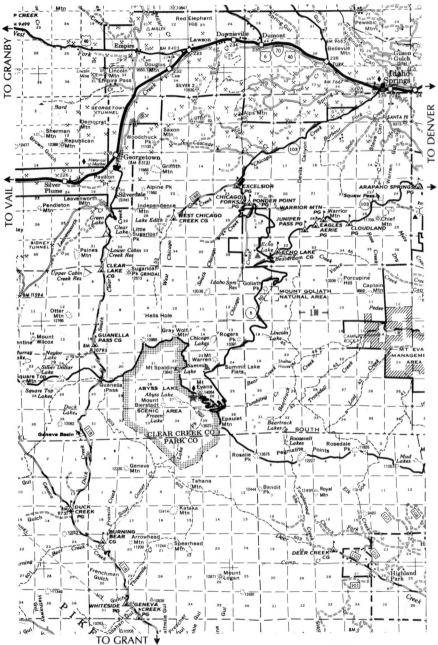

*Courtesy of USDA Forest Service*

# GLENWOOD SPRINGS DISTRICT

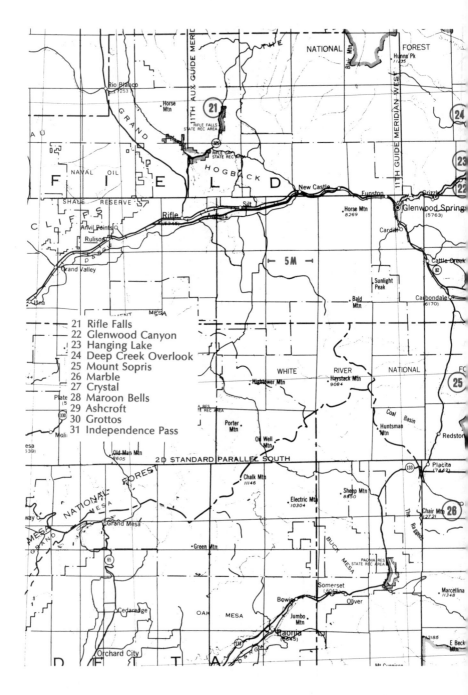

21 Rifle Falls
22 Glenwood Canyon
23 Hanging Lake
24 Deep Creek Overlook
25 Mount Sopris
26 Marble
27 Crystal
28 Maroon Bells
29 Ashcroft
30 Grottos
31 Independence Pass

# GLENWOOD SPRINGS DISTRICT

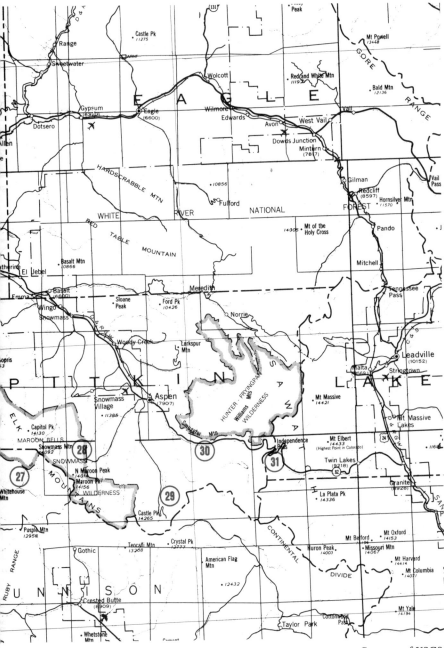

*Courtesy of USGS*

# 21 RIFLE FALLS

TYPE: Plateau Scenery/Geologic
ADMINISTRATION: Public land—Rifle Gap and Falls State Park
QUALITY: Scenic
ACCESS: Paved road
FACILITIES: Campgrounds/Picnic areas
TIME NEEDED: Half day
BEST VISIT: Spring to fall
BEST PHOTO: Midday
ELEVATION: 6,600 feet (top of falls)
REFERENCE: Rifle
MAP: State highway map
White River National Forest visitor map
USGS TOPO: Rifle Falls 7.5' (1966)
USGS COUNTY: Garfield County Sheet 4 of 5 (1975)

Dropping a distance of about 50 feet, these multiple falls provide an unusually wet environment in this part of the state. The Rifle area is part of the plateau region of Colorado, generally considered to be dry and barren. In fact, oil shale is practically the only industry in the vicinity. East Rifle Creek, however, forms a narrow canyon just north of Rifle that supplies enough year-round water to sustain a lush and varied plant community. At the base of the falls, you can often see ferns, mosses, and numerous flowers in bloom.

The falls are created by the waters of East Rifle Creek dropping over a wide travertine dam. Travertine is formed when dissolved calcium carbonate is precipitated out of a stream. Here, East Rifle Creek flows through Rifle Box Canyon which is composed primarily of Leadville limestone. Calcium carbonate and other minerals are dissolved from the canyon's limestone walls. This travertine dam, like many limestone formations, provides an environment for caves. A sign along the trail in Rifle Falls State Park identifies the location of the falls as well as several of the small caves. The cave entrances are scattered along the base of the travertine and limestone formations. These caves are ideal for people who have never been inside a cave to explore. They are short and easy to reach and contain no pits or other hazards. A flashlight is all that you need to explore these small caverns.

One of the larger caves, Rifle Cave, has a walk-in entrance with about a hundred feet of passageways. The main room to the north is a spacious 50 feet long by 25 feet wide. The cave contains caramel- to orange-colored flowstone formations. To the left, just inside the entrance, is a short network of tight crawlways. The entrance is about 100 yards north (around to the right) of the falls at the base of the cliff formation. Another cave, Rifle Falls Cave, is just 50 feet south (around to the left) of the falls. It offers fewer than 75 feet of passageways but has two small rooms. You have to negotiate a tight squeeze at the entrance but it's roomy once you're inside. This cave once had a high water level, which is indicated by a dark ring and formations of a

# 21 RIFLE FALLS

Rifle Falls form an unexpectedly wet environment in this normally dry region.

A flashlight is all that is needed to explore the Rifle Falls Caves.

# 21 RIFLE FALLS

deeper color below the ring. The walls are lined with a formation that resembles popcorn.

Rifle Falls is part of the Rifle Gap and Falls State Recreation Area, for which a state parks pass is required. To enter this area, you must pass through Rifle Gap. This large opening in the Grand Hogback provides drainage for Rifle Creek. It was also the site of the short-lived Valley Curtain, an artistic "sculpture" perpetrated by the internationally known artist Cristo Javachek. The curtain, $700,000 worth of orange nylon fabric, was stretched between the curved valley floor and a cable that linked the two crests of the gap. The project, completed in August 1972, was destroyed within 24 hours by winds typical of the area.

Rifle Mountain Park, farther north on Colorado 325, is also worth a visit. This park offers camping, picnicking, and sightseeing. It is in a very narrow and deep canyon cut from Leadville limestone. This canyon is quite scenic and has several interesting limestone formations of its own. The road that continues beyond this park (northeast from East Rifle Creek) and climbs toward the White River Plateau (Forest Road 835) is not recommended for passenger cars.

**DIRECTIONS:** Take exit 90 <0.0> for Rifle off Interstate 70. Follow Colorado 13 and 789 north toward Rifle by crossing the Colorado River. Do not turn left onto Colorado 13 which bypasses Rifle; continue straight through downtown. At the north end of Rifle you rejoin Colorado 13 (go straight) and continue to the junction <3.8> of Colorado 325. Turn right (north) at this intersection and follow Colorado 325, ignoring the numerous side roads. Continue through Rifle Gap <7.0>, a break in the Grand Hogback and site of the Valley Curtain. Continue over the rock- and earth-filled Silt Project/Rifle Gap Dam <7.8> and stay on paved Highway 325. Continue to a side road <13.4> that leaves to the right (east) marked by a large sign reading "Entering Rifle Falls State Park." Turn right onto this road, which leads a short distance into a campground to a sign displaying a map of the area. After studying the map to become oriented, turn left and head north as far as the road will allow. You must walk the short distance farther north to the falls and their nearby caves.

If you wish to visit Rifle Mountain Park, return to Colorado 325, turn right, and travel north. The park is seven miles farther along the highway. The route takes you past the Rifle Falls State Fish Hatchery just above the falls.

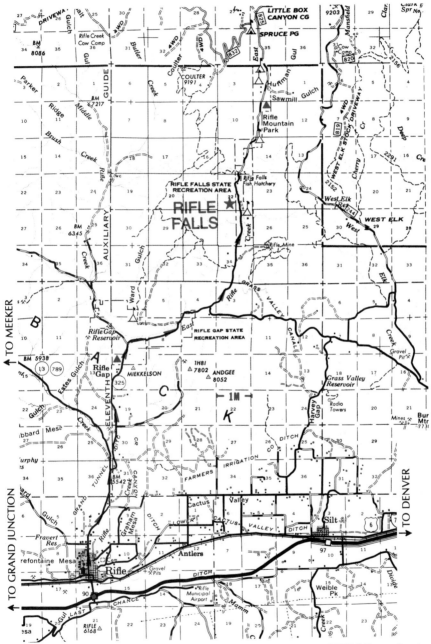

*Courtesy of USDA Forest Service*

# 22 GLENWOOD CANYON

**TYPE:** Plateau Scenery/Geologic
**ADMINISTRATION:** White River National Forest
**QUALITY:** Very scenic
**ACCESS:** Paved road/Bike trail
**FACILITIES:** Picnic areas/Rest rooms at Hanging Lake trailhead
**TIME NEEDED:** One hour
**BEST VISIT:** Spring to fall
**BEST PHOTO:** Morning
**ELEVATION:** 5,960 feet (highway at middle of canyon)
**REFERENCE:** Glenwood Springs
**MAP:** State highway map
White River National Forest visitor map
**USGS TOPO:** Shoshone 7.5' (1961)
Glenwood Springs 7.5' (1961)
**USGS COUNTY:** Garfield County Sheet 5 of 5 (1975)

Glenwood Canyon is thought by some to be most beautiful of all Colorado's canyons. It is indeed scenic, and it's one of the most heavily visited canyons, intentionally or not, in the state. This visitation results from the interstate highway and rail line constructed through the canyon. In 1944, Cyrus Osborn, then head of the Electromotive Division of General Motors, enjoyed this beauty from the cab of a locomotive. He was so impressed by the view that he pondered the effect a glass-topped passenger car would have on its occupants. His idea led to the invention of the Vista Dome passenger liner.

The canyon is 15 miles long and reaches a depth of over 1,800 feet at its midpoint. Sedimentary layers have been sliced by the Colorado River as it cuts through the southern portion of the relatively flat White River Plateau. The younger (higher) layers include Leadville limestone, a vertical-wall and cave-forming sediment, 250 feet thick, that was laid down during the Mississippian period (350 millon years ago); Devonian gray-green limestone; and brown Ordovician dolomite. The older rocks include light and dark brown banded Cambrian quartzite as well as an exposure of coarse Precambrian granite (over 600 million years old).

About halfway through the canyon, there is a rest area at the trailhead for Hanging Lake (see site 23). Farther downstream is a dam built to divert water into the Shoshone Intake. This water is carried by a buried conduit to the Shoshone Power Plant, a small hydroelectric station within the canyon. During seasons of reduced river flow, the stretch of riverbed between the intake and the power plant is virtually dry. Watch for kayakers practicing through the canyon.

**DIRECTIONS:** Glenwood Canyon is located on Interstate 70 between exits 119 (for Noname) and 133 (for Dotsero) east of Glenwood Springs.

Glenwood Canyon provides a scenic passageway for the Colorado River.

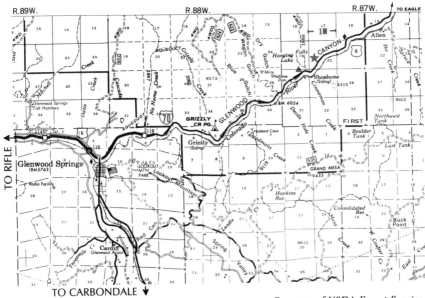

*Courtesy of USDA Forest Service*

# 23 HANGING LAKE

TYPE: Plateau Scenery/Geologic
ADMINISTRATION: White River National Forest
QUALITY: Extremely scenic
ACCESS: Paved road and hike
FACILITIES: Rest rooms and picnic area at trailhead
TIME NEEDED: Half day
BEST VISIT: Spring to fall
BEST PHOTO: Midday
ELEVATION: 7,180 feet (lake surface)
REFERENCE: Glenwood Springs
MAP: State highway map
White River National Forest visitor map
USGS TOPO: Shoshone 7.5' (1961)
USGS COUNTY: Garfield County Sheet 5 of 5 (1975)

Hanging Lake earns its name from its awkward position on the side of a canyon. The lake is contained in a 500-foot-wide bowl made of travertine deposited over the centuries. The geologic fault forming Deadhorse Canyon caused the original lake bed to drop away, leaving this bowl suspended on the sheer east wall of the canyon. The rocks that constitute the surrounding sedimentary layers of the White River Plateau are largely limestones. This provides the source of dissolved calcium carbonate and other minerals that form travertine when precipitated out of solution. The East Fork of Deadhorse Creek carries these dissolved minerals to Hanging Lake. As the lake's water spills over the travertine rim of the bowl, more travertine is slowly added, thus raising the rim of the lake. The shallow lake now sits atop a huge pedestal of travertine that has built up against the east wall of the canyon.

Water flows into the lake from a series of small waterfalls. These falls are scattered all along the upper rim about 20 feet above the lake and make a very photogenic backdrop. The crystalline coloration of the lake results from dissolved minerals. A wooden walkway skirts the rim of the lake to protect the formation and to provide easy access. A wide-angle lens may be handy for photographing the lake. If you're part mountain goat and part crazy, the east wall of the canyon can be scaled to provide a bird's eye view of the lake.

Spouting Rock is above Hanging Lake and can be reached by a spur trail leading uphill just before you get to the lake. This side trail is marked by an engraved wooden sign (easy to miss) identifying the Spouting Rock trail. Spouting Rock is simply an opening about halfway up an inward-sloping cliff from which a surprising amount of water flows. The issuing water completely clears the host wall, making it possible to walk behind this flow without getting wet. Both the lake and Spouting Rock are fed by the waters of the East Fork of Deadhorse Creek and by waters that flow just below the surface through the layers of limestone.

The trail to Hanging Lake begins at a rest area on old US 6 in Glenwood

Note that the water from Spouting Rock drops 30 feet from a hole in the cliff face, not from the cliff top.

# 23  HANGING LAKE

Canyon. The Forest Service has supplied an information sign at the trailhead with data on the area and a copy of the White River National Forest visitor map. The sign warns that this area is closed to fishing, hunting, camping, swimming, motorized vehicles, campfires, and pets on trails. The display also contains some photographs of Hanging Lake and Spouting Rock. The trail is only 1.5 miles long (one way) but gains 1,000 feet in elevation. The resulting steep grade is very demanding for all who are not in good physical condition. Be sure to keep left where a side trail to Coffee Pot Springs (marked by a sign) leaves Deadhorse Creek Canyon. Allow an hour for the trip up and half an hour for the return trip. This effort will be rewarded when you reach the special beauty of the lake and unique Spouting Rock. You may wish to carry some water on this hike.

**DIRECTIONS:** At the time of this revision Interstate 70 was under construction within Glenwood Canyon. When I-70 is completed, exit 125 will provide access for east bound visitors to the Hanging Lake trailhead (no access for west bound traffic). Until I-70 is completed, use the following directions.

From Glenwood Springs, proceed east on I-70 toward Glenwood Canyon. Continue past exit 119 <0.0> for Noname, entering the canyon on old US 6. Continue past the Shoshone Power Plant <4.3> and the Shoshone Intake and Dam <6.8>. Just east of the intake on old US 6 is a large turnout <7.4> on the left (north) side of the road. Park in this area and walk toward a side canon in the north wall of Glenwood Canyon to find the trailhead. Rest rooms and picnic tables are near the trailhead.

Several waterfalls pour over travertine rims into Hanging Lake.

# 23 HANGING LAKE

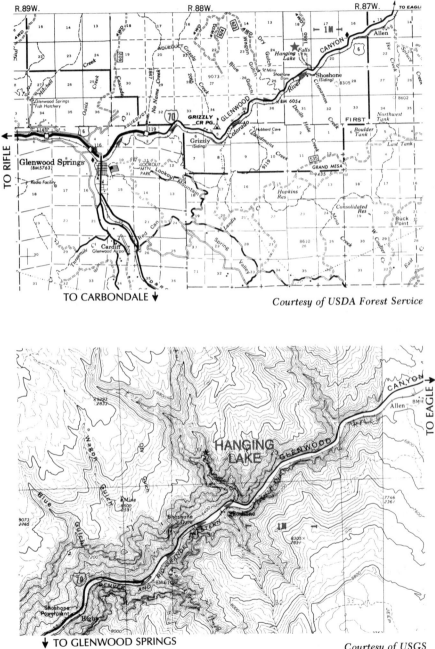

Courtesy of USDA Forest Service

TO RIFLE

TO CARBONDALE

TO GLENWOOD SPRINGS

Courtesy of USGS

TO EAGLE

# 24  DEEP CREEK OVERLOOK

**TYPE:** Plateau Scenery/Geologic
**ADMINISTRATION:** White River National Forest
**QUALITY:** Scenic
**ACCESS:** Good dirt road
**FACILITIES:** Nearby campground
**TIME NEEDED:** Half hour
**BEST VISIT:** Early summer to fall
**BEST PHOTO:** Morning to midday
**ELEVATION:** 9,980 feet
**REFERENCE:** Gypsum
**MAP:** State highway map
White River National Forest visitor map
**USGS TOPO:** Broken Rib Creek 7.5' (1974)
**USGS COUNTY:** Garfield County Sheet 5 of 5 (1975)
Eagle County Sheet 1 of 4 (1977)

Deep Creek has sliced a canyon 2,300 feet deep between Deep Lake and the Colorado River. The canyon, 18 miles long and a mile wide at the overlook, is cut through the White River Plateau, which is made of sedimentary layers. The highest (youngest) layer is composed of shales laid down during the Pennsylvanian period (300 million years ago). This material forms the surface of the plateau. Immediately below the rim of Deep Creek Canyon is an exposed layer of Leadville limestone that forms nearly vertical walls up to 250 feet tall. Steeply sloping strata below include Devonian limestone and shale (390 million years old), Ordovician dolomite (480 million years old), and Cambrian quartzite (560 million years old). Precambrian granite (older than 600 million years) underlies the entire plateau.

The thick layer of Leadville limestone provides an ideal environment for the formation of solution caves. This type of cave develops when limestone is dissolved by dilute carbonic acid, the combination of ground water and atmospheric carbon dioxide. The greatest concentration of caves in the state is found in the Leadville limestone layer of the White River Plateau. Groaning Cave, suspected of being the most extensive cave in Colorado with an estimated 12 miles of passageways, is located nearby. This particular cave has been gated to preserve the fragile speleothems (formations) contained within. Entrances to several caves open into Deep Creek Canyon from the layer of Leadville limestone just below the north and south rims. Because these entrances are generally located in a vertical face high on the walls of this steep canyon, access is usually both difficult and dangerous. With binoculars, you should be able to spot several openings high on the north wall of the canyon.

The large tree near the northeastern corner of the parking area is a bristlecone pine. This tree has been dated to the year 1297 by dendrochronology, the science of counting tree rings. The trail system that crosses the Flat Tops Wilderness north of this location is believed to be part of an

Deep Creek courses through this canyon 2,300 feet below the overlook.

# 24 DEEP CREEK OVERLOOK

extensive network originally established by the Ute Indians. The White River Plateau was most likely a productive hunting ground. In addition to fine views of Deep Creek Canyon, this trip offers wide-ranging vistas of the surrounding distant countryside.

**DIRECTIONS:** From Gypsum, proceed west on Interstate 70 and take exit 133 for Dotsero. Continue west on the access road that parallels I-70 on its north side. After driving over the bridge that crosses the Colorado River, you will come to a stop sign at a T-intersection <0.0>. Turn right at this junction and head north on the road that follows the west bank of the Colorado River. Just beyond this turn you should pass a sign that gives mileages for Sweetwater (17 miles) and Burns (23 miles). Continue on this paved road to the junction <1.8> with a side road to the left (west) marked by a sign that identifies this as Coffee Pot Road and gives mileages for Coffee Pot Campground (17 miles) and Deep Lake (29 miles). A nearby Forest Service sign asks that property rights be respected because the public right-of-way for this road crosses private property. Turn left onto this gravel road and continue past a BLM sign <2.8> indicating public land. The road actually crosses from public to private land and back several times before reaching the National Forest boundary on top of the plateau.

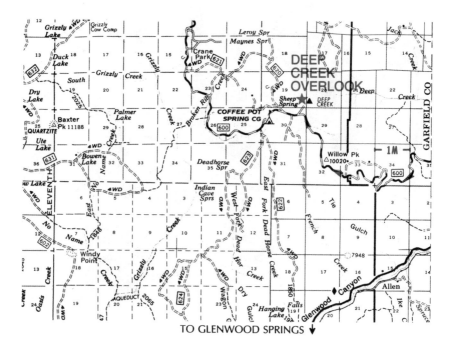

TO GLENWOOD SPRINGS ↓

# 24 DEEP CREEK OVERLOOK

The road zigzags around some interesting rock spires <3.9> and begins its curving climb to the top of the White River Plateau. It is reasonably wide but often rippled and dusty. Just before one of the switchbacks, the road heads straight toward a view <8.1> of Deep Creek Canyon. Several good views <10.5> can be seen toward the south, including the Colorado River, Glenwood Canyon, and the mountaintops along the Roaring Fork Valley near Aspen. The top of the plateau <12.6> is a good place to view the south and east. The National Forest boundary <14.5> is marked by a cattle guard, and a small sign <14.8> identifies this road as Forest Route 600. Continue past a brown White River National Forest sign <15.1> to a junction <17.2> with a dirt road to the right (north) marked by a brown sign identifying it as the access for Deep Creek Overlook. Turn right onto this road and follow it to a square parking area <17.6> on the southern rim of Deep Creek Canyon. If the road is muddy, you should leave your vehicle parked at the side of the gravel road and walk the short distance to the overlook.

There are two fenced overlooks at the canyon rim. One can be reached by walking north toward the canyon, then east and down the hill along a path that leads out onto a rock promontory jutting into the canyon. You can find the other overlook by walking parallel to the rim of the canyon from the west end of the parking area until you approach a fenced area. Small information signs are attached to the fences of both overlooks.

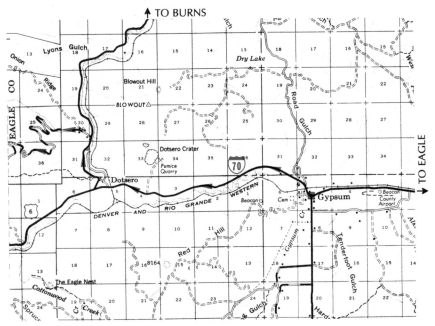

*Courtesy of USDA Forest Service*

# 25 MOUNT SOPRIS

TYPE: Mountain Scenery
ADMINISTRATION: White River National Forest
QUALITY: Scenic
ACCESS: Paved road
FACILITIES: Nearby campgrounds
TIME NEEDED: Quarter hour
BEST VISIT: Spring to fall
BEST PHOTO: Afternoon
ELEVATION: 12,953 feet (summit)
REFERENCE: Carbondale
MAP: State highway map
White River National Forest visitor map
USGS TOPO: Mount Sopris 7.5' (1961)
USGS COUNTY: Pitkin County Sheet 1 of 2 (1975)

The symmetrical hulk of Mount Sopris stands guard above the confluence of the Crystal and Roaring Fork rivers. This mountain actually has a twin summit: West Sopris Peak and Sopris Peak, both at 12,953 feet, are connected by a saddle that dips to 12,660 feet. The apex of the mountain stands over 6,000 feet above the surrounding valley floor. Mount Sopris is an igneous intrusion of a crystalline rock called quartz monzonite. The large area of broken rock that slopes down the face of the northern peak is known as a rock glacier, a field of boulders that creeps slowly downhill as a unit with much the same effect as an ice glacier.

The first recorded expedition to reach the Crystal River Valley was organized by Richard Sopris. The fifteen-man party departed from Denver on July 1, 1860, and explored as far as the Crystal River Valley in search of precious ore. Finding little success, the group returned to the Colorado River (near present Glenwood Springs) by the Roaring Fork River Valley. The expedition members named Mount Sopris in honor of their leader. The area was later visited in 1873 and 1874 by the better-known Hayden survey led by Dr. Ferdinand V. Hayden as part of his geologic exploration of the Colorado Territory.

The drive south on Colorado 133 between Carbondale and Marble takes you through the scenic Crystal River Valley. Part of this valley is cut through the richly colored sandstone and shale of the reddish Maroon Formation. This region is underlaid by several large deposits of coal that have provided industry for the residents of the valley since the turn of the century.

**DIRECTIONS:** From Glenwood Springs, proceed south on Colorado 82 to its junction with Colorado 133. Turn right (south) at this intersection <0.0> toward Carbondale. Continue south on Colorado 133 slightly beyond Carbondale to a small gravel turnout <3.2> on the right (west) side of the road. A second turnout <3.3> is also on the right. This spot offers a photogenic view of Mount Sopris to the southeast.

Mount Sopris is one of the most frequently photographed peaks in Colorado.

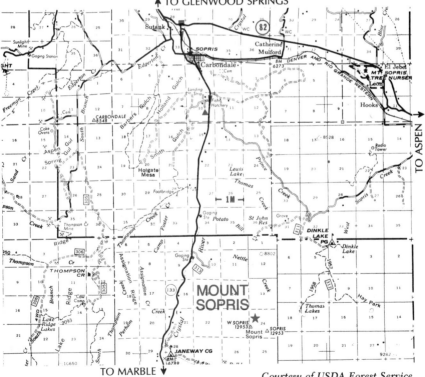

Courtesy of USDA Forest Service

# 26  MARBLE

| | |
|---|---|
| **TYPE:** | Mountain Scenery/Geologic/Historic |
| **ADMINISTRATION:** | Private land/Public land—Marble City Park |
| **QUALITY:** | Extremely scenic |
| **ACCESS:** | Paved road (mill)/Planned new road (quarry) |
| **FACILITIES:** | Rest room and picnic tables at mill site |
| **TIME NEEDED:** | One day |
| **BEST VISIT:** | Early summer to fall |
| **BEST PHOTO:** | Morning to midday |
| **ELEVATION:** | 7,950 feet |
| **REFERENCE:** | Marble |
| **MAP:** | State highway map |
| | White River National Forest visitor map |
| **USGS TOPO:** | Marble 7.5' (1960) |
| **USGS COUNTY:** | Gunnison County Sheet 1 of 6 (1975) |
| | Gunnison County Sheet 2 of 6 (1976) |

Geologic forces near Marble have created a vast supply of the material for which this town is named. A thick stratum of Leadville limestone has been metamorphosed by an igneous intrusion to form a dome of marble. It is exposed in veins along the slopes of Whitehouse and Treasure mountains south of the town. This particular marble is valued because of its strength, purity, flawlessness, glistening white color, and occasionally mottled veins of various pastel hues. For marble of construction quality, this is one of the largest and finest deposits in the world. The northern valley walls opposite the marble deposits are made of shales. These steep and unstable slopes have caused mud flows that have nearly destroyed the town.

George Yule, prospecting for precious metals, was among the first to discover the marble in the 1870s. The town started from the search for gold and silver, but its final name and temporary prosperity came from this crystalline white rock. Many quarries were opened above the 9,000-foot contour of the mountain; the best known of these was the Colorado Yule Marble Company, established just after 1900. A marble mill, then the largest finishing plant in the world, was built at the southern edge of town near the Crystal River. Experienced marble craftsmen were imported from Italy to ensure the finest finished product. Transportation of the cut marble was always one of the major challenges. Before the railroad reached Marble, the rock was moved to the railhead by wagon and sled. The difficulties of moving the raw material to the mill becomes apparent after you visit the quarries.

Marble quarried here was used in a variety of public structures. The Lincoln Memorial was constructed from over a million dollars' worth (1914 prices) of Colorado marble. Government buildings in San Francisco, Denver, and other locations were built from this material. The most famous monument to receive Colorado marble was the Tomb of the Unknown Soldier, sculpted from the single largest piece of marble ever quarried in the

The wooden structure was once part of the rigging used to hoist large blocks of marble from the quarry opening.

Near the mill, the Crystal River is strewn with marble fragments.

The interior of one of the quarry openings bears the scars of the quarrying process.

Yule Creek forms a small cascade over natural steps of pure marble.

world. The 100-ton block required over a year of effort to extract it from the mountain. In the rough form of the final monument (pared to 55 tons), it was shipped to the Vermont Marble Company in New England for final polishing and then to Arlington National Cemetery near the nation's capital. The quarries have been inactive for years, but there are plans to reopen them during the 1990s.

The mill is now a national historic site maintained by the town as a city park. The machinery has largely been removed, but remnants of worked marble as well as support columns and walls built of marble remain. The old factory ruins are fascinating to wander through. It is unlawful to remove or deface any of the marble found in this area. There is a rest room and a picnic table at the mill site.

The quarries, high on the mountain south of the mill, are on private property, but public visitation is allowed (at the time of this revision). Remains of the once large Yule quarry provide hours of entertainment as you explore, enjoy the scenery, and contemplate past activities. You can walk into several openings of the marble quarries along the west side of Yule Creek. You should exercise caution where the floor drops away to the depths of the quarry pits inside the mountain. Parts of buildings, wooden supports, and rigging once used in the mining operation are still outside the quarry portals. Scraps and broken blocks of crystalline rock slope toward Yule Creek. Adjacent to the quarry area, Yule Creek forms a classic, natural waterfall over a pure marble outcropping. Much marble remains in the mountain. Veins can be seen all the way to the summit of Treasure Mountain, east of the quarry site. Please do not remove any marble.

**DIRECTIONS:** From Glenwood Springs, proceed south on Colorado 82. Turn right (south) onto Colorado 133 at its junction <0.0> with Highway 82. Continue south on this road, which follows the scenic Crystal River Valley. A historical marker <17.5> is located in front of the charcoal kilns at the town of Redstone. Farther on, turn left on a paved side road <22.5> marked with a sign indicating this turn for Marble. This road, Gunnison County 3, leads past the Bogan Flats Campground <24.1> to the town of Marble, where it becomes Park Street. Just before passing the Marble General Store, turn right (south) onto Third Street <28.6> (sign) for the mill site. Stop at the mill site parking area <28.7> to visit the mill.

Just south of this parking area is a sturdy new bridge crossing the Crystal River. Plans exist to replace the 3.9 miles of four-wheel-drive road from here to the quarry in 1990 with a high quality hauling road (visitation may be restricted during construction). The new road is expected to have numerous turnouts to encourage visitation to the reopened quarries.

Columns of Colorado Yule marble supported an overhead electric crane in the mill.

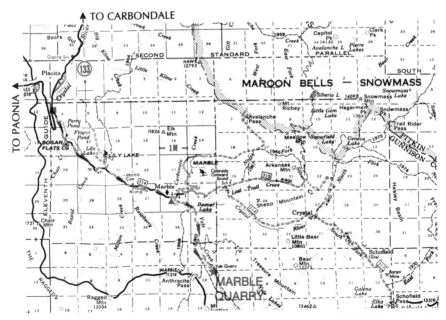

*Courtesy of USDA Forest Service*

# 27  CRYSTAL

TYPE: Mountain Scenery/Historic
ADMINISTRATION: Private land/White River National Forest
QUALITY: Very scenic
ACCESS: Easy 4WD or hike
FACILITIES: None
TIME NEEDED: One hour
BEST VISIT: Early summer to fall
BEST PHOTO: Afternoon
ELEVATION: 8,880 feet (mill)
REFERENCE: Marble
MAP: White River National Forest visitor map
USGS TOPO: Snowmass Mountain 7.5' (1960)
Marble 7.5' (1960)
USGS COUNTY: Gunnison County Sheet 1 of 6 (1975)

Crystal, in the Crystal River Valley, is surrounded by some of Colorado's most scenic mountain topography. The town is situated at the junction of the north and south forks of the Crystal River, where the river continues west, away from town. This area is boxed in by Sheep Mountain to the north, Little Bear Mountain to the south, and Mineral Point, a promontory to the east.

During the early 1880s, development of rich silver ore led to the town's founding. Access to Crystal was originally over Schofield Pass from Crested Butte. The town's inaccessibility and severe winters have always made life difficult for the few year-round occupants. During its boom, Crystal had a hotel, several stores, two newspapers, a few saloons, and a post office, but its population averaged only 500.

The area mines produced silver, lead, and zinc, but transportation costs over Schofield Pass were prohibitive. Mining thrived only after a road was built through the Crystal River Valley to Marble. The town was represented at the 1893 Chicago World's Fair by a rich sample of silver ore from the Black Queen Mine. The silver panic of 1893 brought Crystal's mining activity to a standstill. Even though the Lead King Mine continued to produce into the twentieth century, the town never recovered from this economic catastrophe.

One of the most picturesque historic structures in the state is just west of Crystal. A power station dating back to 1892, it is perched on the southern bank of the Crystal River, atop a rock hogback that crosses the river and forms a low waterfall. When the building was in use, a dam, constructed immediately upstream from the hogback, brought the river level to the base of the structure. Water was channeled near the building and down the wooden enclosed penstock on the hogback's face to the river below. This hydro-power compressed air to power the Sheep Mountain Tunnel Mine drills as well as other mines in the area. Though this building is now somewhat dilapidated, its historic form and dramatic setting lure photog-

This beautiful old building is one of the most photographed historic structures in Colorado.

# 27 CRYSTAL

raphers from all over the world. The structure has seen sporadic restoration in hopes of lengthening its lifespan.

Crystal is most easily reached by a road that follows an old wagon road from the town of Marble through the Crystal River Valley. Though this road is not well suited for passenger cars, it provides an easy trail to follow with relatively few elevation changes along its scenic route. There are no facilities at Crystal, and the town's buildings are privately owned and still occupied.

**DIRECTIONS:** From Glenwood Springs, proceed south on Colorado 82 to its junction with Colorado 133. Turn right (south) at this intersection <0.0> and continue on Highway 133 toward the town of Marble (see site 26). Turn left (east) onto a paved road <22.5> indicated by a sign as the way to Marble. Follow this road to the town and continue past the general store. Stay on the paved road as it winds its way through town by first turning left onto Second Street <28.7>, right onto State Street <28.75>, left onto West First Street <28.8>, right on West Main Street <28.85>, followed by a left <29.05>, and, finally, a right at the next intersection <29.1>.

You now leave the main part of town and drive around the northern edge of Beaver Lake, identified by a sign <29.3> as a state fishing area. Continue on this good graveled road to the beginning of a long, steep hill <30.0>. Drive up the hill on this one-lane road with few turnouts. Continue climbing to an intersection <30.8> where only a few parking spaces are available. This intersection is marked by a brown sign that identifies the road leading uphill as Forest Route 315 and the road downhill as Forest Route 314. The sign further cautions: four-wheel-drive vehicles only. It is not recommended that passenger cars proceed beyond this point, but I do recommend that you take the enjoyable 3.9-mile walk to Crystal.

The road to Crystal is the one that goes downhill (Road 314). Even though this route is labeled as four-wheel-drive only, it is usually passable by two-wheel-drive pickup trucks. Proceed down this road, cross a small bridge <30.9>, and continue past Lizard Lake <31.1> to the beginning <31.3> of a one-lane shelf road high above the Crystal River. The road descends to the river <31.6> and closely follows its northern bank along the distance to Crystal. Cross a talus slope <32.5>, continue past some old stonework <33.2> on the left, and you will eventually come to the scenic old generation station <34.5> on the south side of the Crystal River. Crystal <34.7> is just beyond this structure and is still inhabited. Because these buildings are privately owned and occupied, please do not disturb the residents; stay on the main street. The four-wheel-drive road continues through town and on to Crested Butte over Schofield Pass.

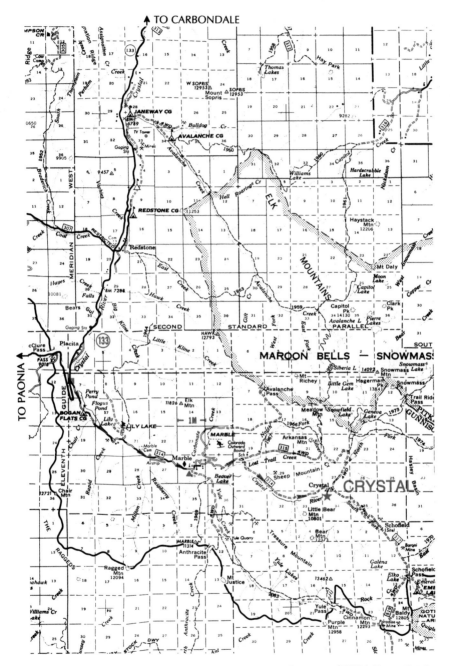

*Courtesy of USDA Forest Service*

# 28 MAROON BELLS

| | |
|---:|:---|
| **TYPE:** | Mountain Scenery/Geologic |
| **ADMINISTRATION:** | White River National Forest |
| **QUALITY:** | Extremely scenic |
| **ACCESS:** | Paved road |
| **FACILITIES:** | Campgrounds/Picnic areas/Shuttle bus |
| **TIME NEEDED:** | One hour |
| **BEST VISIT:** | Early summer to fall |
| **BEST PHOTO:** | Morning |
| **ELEVATION:** | 9,580 feet (Maroon Lake) |
| **REFERENCE:** | Aspen |
| **MAP:** | State highway map |
| | White River National Forest visitor map |
| **USGS TOPO:** | Maroon Bells 7.5' (1960) |
| **USGS COUNTY:** | Pitkin County Sheet 1 of 2 (1975) |

Renderings of the Maroon Bells appear on post cards, calendars, stationery, placemats, posters, books, magazines, and just about every other medium suitable for a color photograph. For many, this is the single image that best represents Colorado. This reputation is well deserved, for the Bells are magnificently scenic. Their name was derived from their coloration and form. From the valley, near Maroon Lake, they appear to be a pair of bells seated firmly on the ground.

These peaks are separated by a distance of 2,100 feet, and the connecting saddle dips a mere 235 feet. Maroon Peak, at 14,156 feet, is the 25th-highest mountain in Colorado. North Maroon Peak ranks 50th and is just barely a "fourteener" at 14,014 feet. This pair forms part of the west wall of Maroon Valley, three miles north of West Maroon Pass. Directly east from the Bells is another spectacular crest, Pyramid Peak. At 14,018 feet, it is the 47th-highest in the state. Maroon Lake, part of Maroon Creek dammed by a pair of talus alluvial fans from both valley walls, forms an ideal foreground for the peaks three miles away.

A popular walk is the 1.5-mile Crater Lake Trail (Forest Trail 1975). This well-traveled path leads to another scenic overlook of the Bells and surrounding terrain. In fact, foot trails form an extensive network in this region, which is part of the Maroon Bells-Snowmass Wilderness. This protected area was established in 1933 to preserve the natural beauty of the many high peaks in this portion of the Elk Mountains.

The Bells are made from sedimentary rocks of the Maroon Formation. Formed from sand and mud (eroded material from the ancestral mountains to the west), these layers once reached a thickness of more than 10,000 feet. During the Tertiary period, these sediments were invaded by igneous intrusions. The granite stock of nearby Snowmass Peak and other surrounding igneous features were formed at this time. This upheavel provided the heat and pressure necessary to metamorphose the sedimentary strata of the Maroon Formation. Sandstone from sand and shale from mud were trans-

Maroon Lake forms a reflecting surface for Colorado's best-known mountain scene.

STATE OF COLORADO

formed into quartzite and slate. The slate gives the grayish tint to the deep red quartzite. Both metamorphic rocks are resistant to erosion and have survived as these dramatic peaks. The major uplift of the Sawatch Range has left these layers tilted uphill toward the east.

This mountain pair is burdened with a sinister nickname—the "Deadly Bells"—that results from many climbing disasters on the peaks. Because of variable weather, complicated routes, and the poor quality of the rock, these are two of the most difficult peaks in Colorado to ascend. At least six climbers have been killed and many more injured while trying to scale the Bells. Most injuries are from falling rock. The sedimentary rock that forms these peaks tends to break off more easily than the stable granite of most Colorado mountains. Fritz Stammberger, a German-born mountaineer, has conquered both of the Maroon Peaks in winter. He performed an even more incredible stunt on June 14, 1971. After carefully planning a route along the snow-covered ledges of North Maroon Peak, he climbed to the summit and then skied the route down the north face of the peak in three-quarters of an hour. Only after seeing this mountain can you truly appreciate his feat.

Many people visit Maroon Valley each year. The Forest Service has built rail fences near Maroon Lake to keep spectators on the established trails. To reduce air pollution from private vehicles, a shuttle-bus service was started in 1978. Private cars are barred from the valley during the summer season, and visitors must use the shuttle (unless camping in the valley). While visiting this area, please help preserve its fragile beauty.

**DIRECTIONS:** Proceed west on Colorado 82 from Aspen. Just beyond the main part of town, a highway bridge crosses Castle Creek <0.0> (identified by a small white sign). Continue past a side road on the right (north) at a stoplight. Turn left at a stoplight <0.4> onto a paved road marked by a sign identifying Aspen Highlands. Immediately after this turn, there is a side road on the left labeled by a sign indicating a left turn for Castle Creek or straight for Maroon Creek. Continue straight at this intersection and pass a sign indicating Maroon Lake (10 miles). Continue to the National Forest check-in station <2.0>. The paved road continues eight miles to Maroon Lake.

If you are visiting during the summer season, you will be required to leave your car at the Aspen Highlands Ski Area parking lot near the check-in station. You can then take a shuttle bus to Maroon Lake. Buses leave from the check-in station on a regular basis while the road is closed to private vehicles (usually 8:30 AM to 5:00 PM). Bus fare is charged per person. Camping is by permit only (available at the check-in station); however, the campgrounds are almost always full. Private vehicles are allowed to use the Maroon Lake road during the off-season or when the shuttle buses are not running (early morning or late in the day).

The Bells are beautiful year-round.

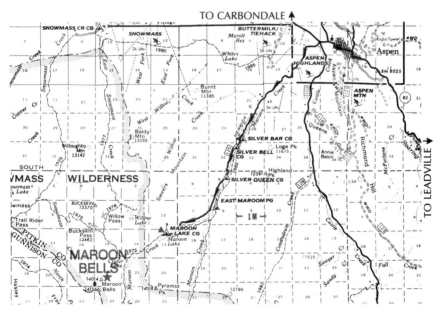

*Courtesy of USDA Forest Service*

# 29  ASHCROFT

TYPE: Mountain Scenery/Historic
ADMINISTRATION: White River National Forest
QUALITY: Scenic
ACCESS: Paved road
FACILITIES: Rest rooms/Picnic area
TIME NEEDED: One hour
BEST VISIT: Early summer to fall
BEST PHOTO: Morning
ELEVATION: 9,498 feet
REFERENCE: Aspen
MAP: State highway map
White River National Forest visitor map
USGS TOPO: Hayden Peak 7.5' (1960)
USGS COUNTY: Pitkin County Sheet 2 of 2 (1976)

Ashcroft is situated along Castle Creek, which parallels Maroon Creek (see site 28). Both creeks feed into the Roaring Fork River just west of Aspen. The townsite, near the head of the valley, is walled in by Hayden Peak (13,561 feet), Cathedral Peak (13,943 feet), and Castle Peak (14,265 feet) to the west; Pearl Mountain (13,362 feet) and Star Peak (13,521 feet) to the south; and Taylor Peak (13,435 feet) and Ashcroft Mountain (12,381 feet) to the east. This area is within the Elk Mountains, just east of the Maroon Bells-Snowmass Wilderness.

Prospectors from the Leadville area began exploring this region in the late 1870s. They were searching for precious metals in the Colorado mineral belt, which crosses this part of the Elk Mountains. During the district's early mining days, Taylor Pass, a rugged saddle in the south end of the valley, was the best access to Castle Valley and the Roaring Fork Valley to the north. Early users of this pass were forced to dismantle their wagons and lower them piece by piece, along with their cargo, over drops of about 40 feet. Because Taylor Pass originally had more traffic than Independence Pass, Ashcroft was more important than Aspen for a few years.

Silver was discovered in this valley by 1879, and prospecting became a serious business. A miners' collective under the guidance of C. B. Culver was formed in June 1880 by 97 valley pioneers. Each prospective member had his choice of contributing either $5.00 or a day's labor and a dollar in cash. This protective organization laid out a townsite with 840 lots to be divided among its members. Log buildings were soon completed on the various lots.

Few residents remained in the settlement through the winter of 1880-81, but the population grew to 500 by the end of the next summer. Ashcroft soon had a public school, a jail, a newspaper, many stores, the usual saloons, and other facilities for the residents. Services included daily mail, telegraphic communication, and stage service to Aspen, Independence, and Leadville. Freight transportation, however, was a problem. Coal had to be hauled over

# 29  ASHCROFT

STATE OF COLORADO

These remaining buildings have been partially restored.

# 29  ASHCROFT

Pearl Pass from Crested Butte, and precious ores from early mining production had to be packed out by way of Taylor and Pearl passes. These were expensive and hazardous routes. Even today, the four-wheel-drive roads following each of these routes offer bone-jarring, hair-raising excitement.

Horace Tabor, already wealthy at this time, built a house in Ashcroft in the fall of 1883. The house was lavishly furnished on the inside, including gold-inlaid wallpaper. He invested heavily in the Montezuma and Tam O'Shanter mines, both in the surrounding mountains, and was instrumental in starting a smelting operation in town. With the arrival of Baby Doe, his new bride, Tabor declared a 24-hour holiday at the local saloons with free drinks for all.

The town reached its zenith in 1885 with a summer population over 1,000, not counting the transient prospectors frequenting the area. By this time Aspen had been founded, and Independence Pass traffic surpassed that of Taylor Pass. In 1887, the railroad reached Aspen. Most of Ashcroft's businesses and residents had moved to Aspen by 1890, and the silver panic of 1893 virtually killed the town. The post office held out until 1912, leaving only a handful of inhabitants to keep the town alive.

In 1937, the Highland Bavarian Corporation obtained title to the town and the surrounding land. They intended to develop the property as part of an alpine ski resort, but World War II interrupted these plans. During the war, this region was used as a training ground by the 10th Mountain Division ski troops from Camp Hale near Leadville. Several movies and television programs have been filmed in the area; among them was the popular 1950s television series, "Sergeant Preston of the Yukon." The townsite was deeded to the United States Forest Service in 1953 by the president of the Highland Bavarian Corporation. Funds from public and private sectors have contributed to the restoration of the present remains.

**DIRECTIONS:** From Aspen, proceed west on Colorado 82. Just outside the main part of town, a highway bridge crosses Castle Creek <0.0> (identified by a small white sign attached to the bridge). Continue straight at a stoplight where a side road joins to the right. Turn left at a stoplight <0.4> onto a paved road marked by a sign identifying Aspen Highlands. Immediately after this turn, there is a side road on the left marked by a sign indicating a left turn for Castle Creek. Turn left at this intersection <0.45> and continue toward Ashcroft (11 miles). Follow this paved road south through Castle Valley to a sign <11.4> indicating a left turn to a Historic Site. Turn left into the graveled parking area. A boardwalk leaves the southern end of the parking area, passes an information sign, and leads to the remains of the town. Rest rooms are at the northern end of the parking area.

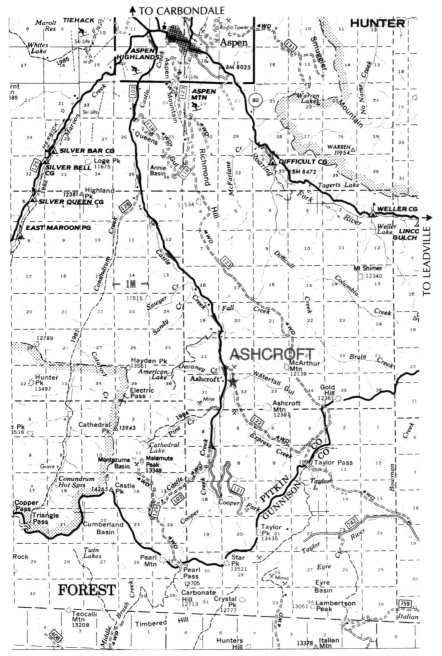

*Courtesy of USDA Forest Service*

# 30 GROTTOS

TYPE: Mountain Scenery/Geologic
ADMINISTRATION: White River National Forest
QUALITY: Scenic
ACCESS: Paved road
FACILITIES: Picnic tables/Rest rooms
TIME NEEDED: One hour
BEST VISIT: Early summer to fall
BEST PHOTO: Midday
ELEVATION: 9,560 feet (surface of Grottos)
REFERENCE: Aspen
MAP: State highway map
White River National Forest visitor map
USGS TOPO: New York Peak 7.5' (1960)
USGS COUNTY: Pitkin County Sheet 2 of 2 (1976)

The Grottos are a series of spacious caverns cut into a large granite outcropping by an earlier course of the Roaring Fork River. The river's route is now slightly to the north, leaving the Grottos relatively dry (although you can sometimes find ice that is protected year-round by the caverns). This large mass of granite has been polished smooth on top by glacial action. The only hint on the outside of the caverns contained within is a narrow slit across the surface, admitting light into the Grottos. You can enter the caverns from an opening at their west end. It is also interesting to explore the remainder of the former riverbed farther upstream to the east.

DIRECTIONS: From Aspen, proceed east on Colorado 82 and pass the Aspen city limit at the east end of town. The city limit sign <0.0> is posted for westbound traffic (coming into Aspen) on Colorado 82. Continue past the White River National Forest sign <3.1> on the left (north) side of the road and past Weller Campground <7.3> to an unmarked graveled side road to the right (south). This is the only side road between Weller Campground and the Lincoln Creek Road. Turn right at this junction <8.3> and follow the graveled road down the hill to a square parking area <8.4>. Cross the footbridge at the south side of the parking area to the south side of the Roaring Fork River. From this end of the bridge, follow the trail east for 360 paces to a point where it crosses a smooth granite rock outcropping that slopes gently downhill to the left (north). Also to the left is a small power line supported by wooden poles. Leave the trail and walk downhill and slightly to the left toward the Roaring Fork River and the highway beyond. After about 50 paces you come to a former stream outlet carved in the granite where you can carefully climb down into the Grottos.

If you are headed west from Independence Pass <0.0>, continue on Colorado 82 past the Lincoln Creek Road <9.8>, marked by a green sign. Farther west, there is a graveled side road to the left. Turn left at this junction <10.7> to reach the parking area.

# 30  GROTTOS

The interior of the Grottos appears unexpectedly large after one has seen the small openings that join the cavern with the outside world.

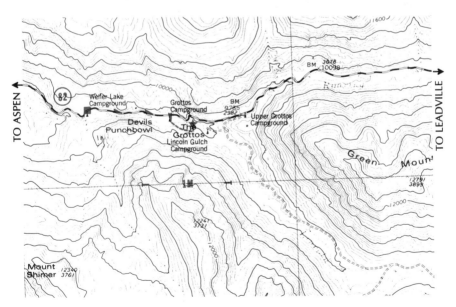

Also see map on page 150.

# 31 INDEPENDENCE PASS

**TYPE:** Mountain Scenery
**ADMINISTRATION:** White River and San Isabel National Forests
**QUALITY:** Very scenic
**ACCESS:** Paved road
**FACILITIES:** Nearby campgrounds
**TIME NEEDED:** Half hour
**BEST VISIT:** Early summer to fall
**BEST PHOTO:** Afternoon
**ELEVATION:** 12,095 feet
**REFERENCE:** Aspen
**MAP:** State highway map
White River National Forest visitor map
**USGS TOPO:** Independence Pass 7.5' (1960)
**USGS COUNTY:** Pitkin County Sheet 2 of 2 (1976)
Lake County (1975)

Independence Pass, at 12,095 feet, is the nation's highest passenger car crossing of the Continental Divide. Though closed most of the year by heavy snows, it is open during summer and early fall, providing the shortest path between Aspen and Leadville on Colorado Highway 82. During the winter, an additional 120 miles must be traveled between those cities by way of Glenwood Springs.

One of the first recorded sightings of the pass was made by Captain Zebulon Pike. He and his party were on a government-sponsored expedition to map out the southern boundary of the Louisiana Purchase, which was in dispute with Spain. From the upper Arkansas Valley, Pike sighted the Independence Pass gap among the lofty Sawatch peaks on December 22, 1806.

The pass was not recognized as an important route until the mining boom of the 1870s. Prospectors fanning out from Leadville in search of new riches occasionally used this crossing, then known as Hunter's Pass. This was a difficult way to reach the Roaring Fork Valley to the west. The popular route was over Cottonwood Pass into Taylor Park and then over Taylor Pass (not much easier than Independence Pass) to Ashcroft (see site 29). From here, it was an easy jaunt down Castle Creek to the Roaring Fork Valley. Because Independence Pass was a more direct route (60 miles instead of 100), it was destined to become an important crossing.

It is said that gold was discovered on Independence Day, July 4, 1879, just four miles west of the pass. The town that began there became known as Independence, and the inhabitants of the Roaring Fork Valley began calling Hunter's Pass by the name Independence Pass. The first trail improvements were completed in the spring of 1880 by the Twin Lakes and Roaring Fork Toll Company. It was now possible, though still not easy, to use horses in crossing the pass—quite an improvement. Competition came from Taylor

The view from Independence Pass encompasses many of the Sawatch peaks east of the Continental Divide.

This marker shows the altitude of one of the highest automobile roads in the country.

# 31 INDEPENDENCE PASS

Pass and Pearl Pass, which linked Ashcroft with Crested Butte, recent recipient of a rail connection. Against this threat, the toll company resolved to complete a wagon road over the pass by the summer of 1881. The road was officially opened between Leadville and Aspen on November 6 of that year.

Despite the ensuing snows, the road was an instant success with a huge volume of freight traffic. When wagons became useless, horse-drawn sleighs were used to cope with the winter conditions. An army of men with shovels was required to keep the road passable, and the tolls reflected this. It is hard to imagine that the pass stayed in nearly constant use through five consecutive winters. During summer, stagecoaches were able to take the carefully banked switchback turns at full speed. Well-trained dogs ran ahead to warn approaching traffic to get out of the way.

A normal journey over the pass required 10 to 25 hours, five changes of horses, and passage through three toll gates. After the railroad reached Aspen in 1888, the pass was used less, and the toll gates were closed. The old wagon road saw little activity until an automobile road over the pass was completed during the 1920s.

The pass is well above timberline and is curiously flat where the highway crosses its crest. The windswept landscape seems somewhat desolate and perpetually chilly, even in the middle of summer. A few small lakes and a parking area are found at the top, where a short path leads to exceptional views of the Sawatch Range to the east. There are also displays about the Continental Divide and the alpine tundra. Sections of Colorado 82 between Aspen and the pass are narrow and winding and may not be suitable for long

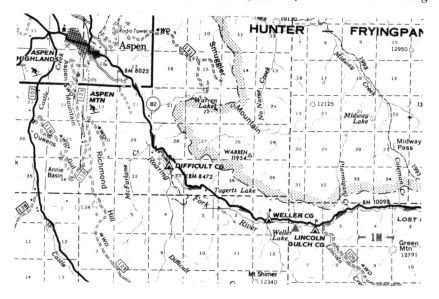

# 31 INDEPENDENCE PASS

vehicles. Worthwhile stops along the route include the ghost town of Independence and the Grottos (see site 30).

**DIRECTIONS:** From Aspen, proceed east on Colorado 82. The city limit sign <0.0> is posted for westbound traffic at the edge of town. Continue east past Weller Campground <7.3>, past a turn <8.3> on the right (south) for the Grottos (see site 30), and beyond Lincoln Creek Road <9.2> marked by a green sign. Proceed past the Braille Nature Trail <11.6> and beyond Lost Man Campground <13.0> to the townsite of Independence <14.8>. You may wish to stop and explore the ghost town, south of the highway.

Continue eastbound on Colorado 82. Near the head of the valley <16.3>, you can see the old pass switchbacks below the present shelf road on the opposite side of the valley. Continue to Independence Pass <19.0> on the Continental Divide. A parking area is provided, and a short path leads past informative signs to a viewpoint looking east.

Colorado 82 drops into the valley of the North Fork of Lake Creek. After reaching the bottom, there is a turnout <25.1> on the right (south) side of the road (marked by a blue "point of interest" sign). This turnout has displays about avalanches, biological zones, and the history of Independence Pass. The highway continues past Twin Peaks Campground <32.8> to a reservoir that is part of the Frying Pan-Arkansas Pump Storage Project. The Visitor Center <38.2> is on the right (south) side of the road. Where Highway 82 joins <42.7> with US 24, a left turn takes you to Leadville and a right turn to Buena Vista.

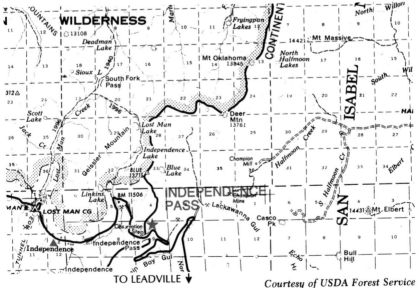

*Courtesy of USDA Forest Service*

# LEADVILLE DISTRICT

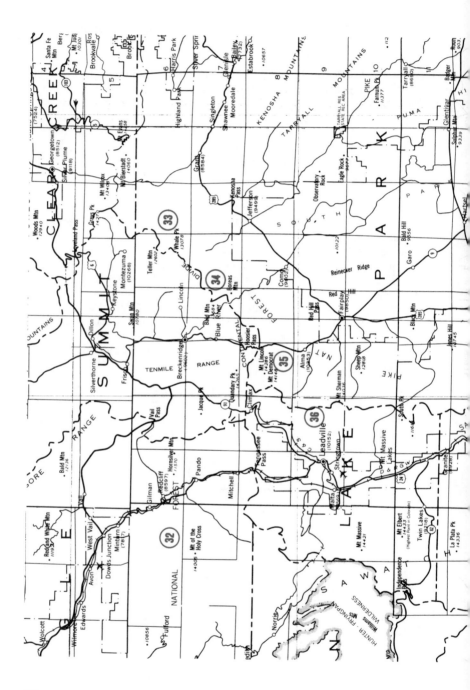

# LEADVILLE DISTRICT

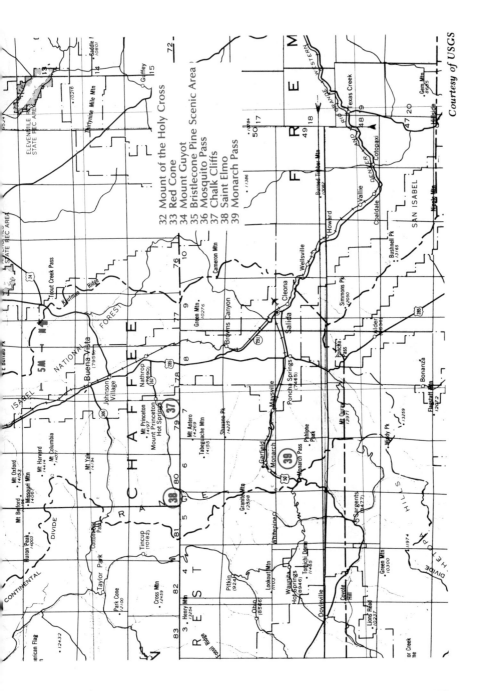

Courtesy of USGS

32 Mount of the Holy Cross
33 Red Cone
34 Mount Guyot
35 Bristlecone Pine Scenic Area
36 Mosquito Pass
37 Chalk Cliffs
38 Saint Elmo
39 Monarch Pass

# 32  MOUNT OF THE HOLY CROSS

TYPE: Mountain Scenery/Historic
ADMINISTRATION: White River National Forest
QUALITY: Extremely scenic
ACCESS: Rough dirt road and hike
FACILITIES: Campground at trailhead
TIME NEEDED: Half day
BEST VISIT: July
BEST PHOTO: Morning
ELEVATION: 14,005 feet (summit)
REFERENCE: Minturn
MAP: State highway map
White River National Forest visitor map
USGS TOPO: Mount of the Holy Cross 7.5' (1970)
USGS COUNTY: Eagle County Sheet 4 of 4 (1975)

Mount of the Holy Cross stands near the end of Holy Cross Ridge, a northeasterly extension from the main Sawatch Range. Like the rest of its neighbors, the mountain is composed of granite gneiss. The cross is formed by vertical and horizontal fissures that intersect symmetrically. Fifteen hundred feet tall and 700 feet wide, the snow-filled cross stands in profound contrast to the mountain's dark background. Because the cross faces northeast, snow protected in its crevices lasts well into summer, long after the more exposed snow has melted away. Notch Mountain, at a height of 13,237 feet, is directly opposite the cross on the east side of East Cross Creek Gulch and forms a natural pedestal for viewing the cross.

Rumors of a mountain, deep in remote terrain, displaying a snowy white cross upon its face were circulated for years by Indians, trappers, and prospectors. The first written mention of the mountain came in 1869 from William Brewer, who had seen the cross from atop Grays Peak, a fair distance to the east. As official photographer to the Hayden surveys of 1870, 1872, and 1873, William Henry Jackson had heard of this cross and was constantly in search of accurate directions to the mountain. One of the activities of the 1873 expedition allowed Jackson to climb Grays Peak. From there, he captured his first glimpse of the elusive mountain. Later that summer, the survey party worked its way to the north side of Tennessee Pass. While in this area, a member of the party sighted the cross from the summit of Mount Powell, a 13,534-foot peak in the Gore Range. On August 23, Jackson and his group managed to climb to the top of Notch Mountain, while Professor Hayden and his group tried to climb the Mount of the Holy Cross to complete a triangulation. Even though the weather precluded all but a fleeting glimpse of the cross, Jackson knew he had reached his goal at long last. It was the next morning—Sunday, August 24, 1873—that Jackson once again reached the top of Notch Mountain and was able to take the first photographs of the cross. Prints were exhibited at the National Centennial Celebration of 1876, making both Jackson and the mountain instantly famous.

Snow-filled crevices form the arms of Mount of the Holy Cross.

# 32  MOUNT OF THE HOLY CROSS

During the 1880s, the area surrounding the mountain underwent a mining boom. Despite this, access to the site remained difficult, and only a few small groups made pilgrimages to the cross. In 1929, President Herbert Hoover signed a proclamation establishing Holy Cross National Monument with an area of 1,392 acres, even though the rough terrain precluded much visitation. The area was closed to the public from 1938 to 1950, when it was part of the Camp Hale military reservation. Due to dwindling visitation, the Park Service never considered it practical to staff a ranger station within the monument's boundaries. By an act of Congress and with the signature of President Harry Truman, Holy Cross National Monument was abolished on August 3, 1950.

Today, a serviceable road allows passenger cars to approach the base of Notch Mountain at its northern end. From there, a healthy hike is required to properly view the cross. Mid-July usually offers the best viewing conditions, when most of the surrounding snow has disappeared, leaving only the arms of the cross full. The best viewing time depends on the previous winter's snowfall and may vary by a month. The cross can also be seen from Shrine Pass, east of Redcliff.

**DIRECTIONS:** Take exit 171 <0.0> off Interstate 70 for Minturn and Leadville. Proceed south on US 24 past the White River National Forest Ranger Station <2.0> in the center of Minturn. Just before starting a series of switchbacks toward the summit of Battle Mountain, turn right (west) at a junction <4.8> with a graveled road that crosses under a pipeline supported by a tall wooden trestle. A sign identifies this as the Tigiwon Road. Continue on this occasionally rough and sometimes muddy dirt road past Tigiwon Campground to the end of the road <13.1>, just beyond Half Moon Campground. Passenger cars can make it if they go slowly over the rough spots.

A sign at the west end of the parking lot area identifies Half Moon Pass Trail. This is the head of Forest Trail 2009. Follow this trail west for 1.7 miles to the saddle of Half Moon Pass, which is identified by a sign. From here, turn left (south), facing the north end of Notch Mountain, and leave the established trail. Start climbing Notch Mountain while traversing to the right (moving around to its west side). Continue this cross-country trek over talus above timberline for another mile or until you are satisfied with the view of Mount of the Holy Cross to the south. Be sure to carry water and weather protection gear on this hike. This is not an easy walk; there is an elevation gain of nearly 2,000 feet. Allow two hours or more each way.

An alternative trail to the summit of Notch Mountain leaves from the southern edge of the parking lot and is marked by a post. The trail (Forest Trail 2001) is 5.5 miles long one way with an elevation gain of 3,000 feet. Allow three hours or more each way. Though this trail is longer and higher, the view from Notch Mountain is directly toward the cross.

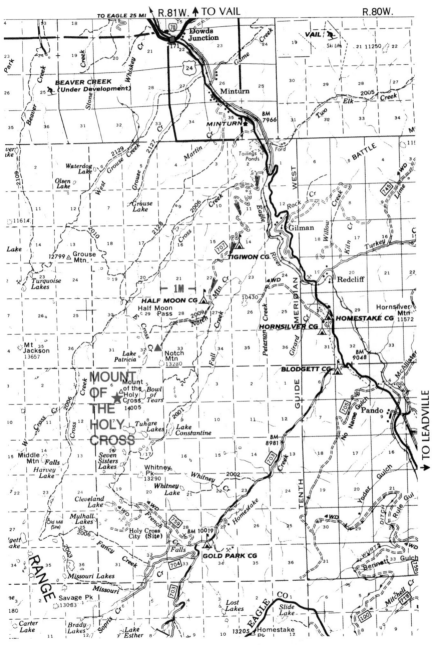

*Courtesy of USDA Forest Service*

# 33  RED CONE

TYPE: Mountain Scenery/Historic
ADMINISTRATION: Pike National Forest/Private land
QUALITY: Scenic
ACCESS: Moderate 4WD
FACILITIES: Nearby campgrounds and picnic areas
TIME NEEDED: Half day
BEST VISIT: Midsummer to late summer
BEST PHOTO: Midday to afternoon
ELEVATION: 12,801 feet (summit)
REFERENCE: Jefferson
MAP: Pike National Forest visitor map
USGS TOPO: Montezuma 7.5' (1974)
Jefferson 7.5' (1958)
USGS COUNTY: Park County Sheet 1 of 4 (1975)
Summit County Sheet 2 of 2 (1977)

Red Cone Peak is just two-tenths of a mile south of the Continental Divide and forms the east wall of upper Handcart Gulch. Handcart Peak (12,518 feet) forms the western wall of this scenic valley. An exciting jeep road climbs the ridge linking these two peaks to Webster Pass (12,096 feet) astride the Continental Divide. (Handcart Gulch drains onto the Atlantic side.) This pass was originally known as Handcart Pass, named after the mode of transport used by an early prospector. The pass was renamed by William and Emerson Webster, who made it a toll freight road in 1878. The route remained in operation for about 10 years and served mining areas near Montezuma to the north. Both Red Cone and Handcart Peak are extremely colorful. The bright red and orange hues result from iron oxide in the rock.

If you are not equipped with a four-wheel-drive vehicle, Red Cone, Handcart Peak, and the shelf road leading to Webster Pass can be seen from US Highway 285 just north of Kenosha Pass. Their unique coloration makes them distinguishable from the surrounding mountains, even from a respectable distance. Binoculars aid the view from the highway.

**DIRECTIONS:** From Jefferson <0.0> on US 285, proceed east toward Kenosha Pass. A turnout <3.6> just below Kenosha Pass <4.4> has a stone historical marker and broad vistas of South Park. Just beyond (north of) the pass, there is a turnout <4.7> on the right (east) side of the road near mile-marker 204. From this turnout, looking straight along the highway (north and slightly west) will help you find Red Cone. Continue downhill on US 285; ignore the first side road <5.9> on the left. Continue to the second side road on the left at an unmarked intersection <8.6> between mile-markers 207 and 208. Turn left onto this dirt road.

Just after this turn, you will encounter a sign warning that Red Cone and Webster Pass roads require four-wheel-drive and may be closed by snows well into August. Continue past a sign <11.2> on the right that

# 33  RED CONE

Upper Handcart Gulch is partially rimmed by Handcart Peak on the Continental Divide.

# 33 RED CONE

identifies the trail to Burning Bear Gulch (a name that conjures up interesting images) and Geneva Park. Go straight at an intersection <11.8> with a road to the left marked as Beaver Creek Road. Continue past Handcart Campground <13.5> to an intersection <13.7> with a road to the left identified by a sign as access to Hall Valley and Gibson Lake Trail. At this junction, continue straight on the route marked as access to Handcart Gulch, Webster Pass, and Red Cone Road.

A sign warns that beyond this point, the road is not maintained and is hazardous to public use; here, the road becomes an honest jeep road. It leads to a T-intersection <13.8> with Red Cone Road to the right and Webster Pass Road to the left. DO NOT take the Red Cone Road, which is an extremely hazardous route that should be attempted only by brave, experienced jeep drivers. Turn left at this T and bear left at the next T-intersection <13.9>. Continue past an interesting mine opening <15.9> on the right (unsafe to go inside) to the base of a rock glacier <16.8> that slopes down from Red Cone. The road continues to a basin at the head of Handcart Gulch, where switchbacks lead to an excitingly narrow shelf road just below Webster Pass (may be closed by snow until late summer). The route down the north side of the pass is an easy four-wheel-drive road (passable by 2WD trucks) that exits onto a good graveled road near Montezuma. This road continues to US 6 near the Keystone ski area.

A rock glacier forms the western slopes of colorful Red Cone.

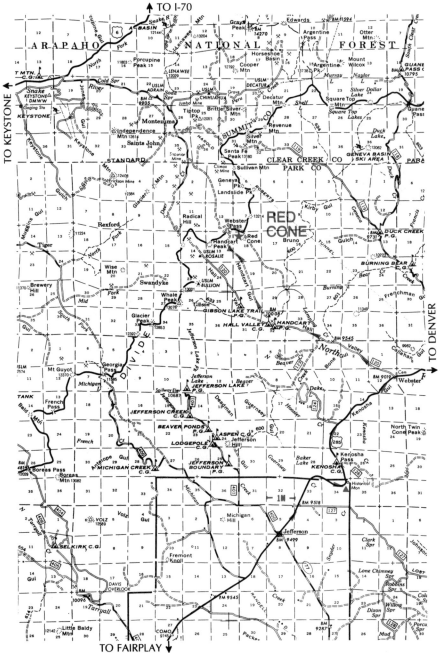

*Courtesy of USDA Forest Service*

# 34  MOUNT GUYOT

**TYPE:** Mountain Scenery/Historic
**ADMINISTRATION:** Pike National Forest
**QUALITY:** Scenic
**ACCESS:** Good dirt road
**FACILITIES:** Nearby campgrounds and picnic areas
**TIME NEEDED:** Half hour
**BEST VISIT:** Midsummer to late summer
**BEST PHOTO:** Morning
**ELEVATION:** 13,370 feet (summit)
**REFERENCE:** Jefferson
**MAP:** Pike National Forest visitor map
**USGS TOPO:** Boreas Pass 7.5' (1957)
**USGS COUNTY:** Park County Sheet 1 of 4 (1975)
Summit County Sheet 2 of 2 (1977)

Mount Guyot, part of the Continental Divide, stands immediately west of Georgia Pass (11,585 feet) which offers views of Mount Guyot, South Park, and the mining area southeast of Dillon. At one time, Georgia Pass received heavy use. With mining successes in the Breckenridge and Dillon areas in the early 1860s, the popular route from Denver was over Kenosha Pass and then over the newly completed wagon road across Georgia Pass. Climbing the South Park side was straightforward, but the descent into the Swan River Valley was difficult. Georgia Pass fell into disuse several years later, as Hoosier Pass, farther to the west, became the route of choice. Today, passenger cars with at least average ground clearance should be able to reach the pass from Jefferson. Other roads lead north and east from the pass to areas of outstanding scenery, but they require a four-wheel-drive vehicle. Several camp and picnic grounds are along the side road to Jefferson Lakes.

**DIRECTIONS:** A large green sign <0.0> on the northwest side of US 285 in Jefferson identifies a road leading to the north as National Forest access for Jefferson and Michigan Creek roads. Take this good dirt road from Jefferson and follow it past a side road <2.0> on the right marked as access to Jefferson Lakes (6 miles). After going straight at that intersection, continue past a sign identifying Michigan Creek Campground (4 miles) to another intersection <2.8>. Take the right fork and, after the curve, pass a Park County 54 sign. Turn left at an intersection <5.4> marked by a sign suggesting left turns for both Michigan Creek Campground (1 mile) and Georgia Pass (7 miles). Continue past Michigan Creek Campground <6.0>, Michigan Creek <6.3>, and French Creek <8.4> while staying on the main graveled road. A good view of Mount Guyot (northwest) is available at a switchback <10.9> where the road narrows a bit. Continue on the main road that climbs as it makes its way to Georgia Pass <12.2>. The roads continuing from the pass, which drop into the Swan River mining area, require a four-wheel-drive vehicle.

Symmetrical Mount Guyot sits astride the Continental Divide at 13,370 feet.

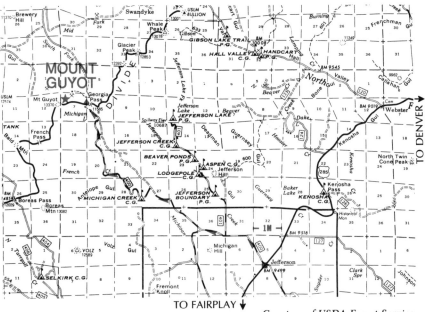

TO FAIRPLAY ↓

*Courtesy of USDA Forest Service*

# 35 BRISTLECONE PINE SCENIC AREA

TYPE: Mountain Scenery/Botanic
ADMINISTRATION: Pike National Forest
QUALITY: Scenic
ACCESS: Dirt road
FACILITIES: None
TIME NEEDED: One hour
BEST VISIT: Midsummer to late summer
BEST PHOTO: Midday
ELEVATION: 11,724 feet (Windy Ridge)
REFERENCE: Fairplay
MAP: Pike National Forest visitor map
USGS TOPO: Alma 7.5' (1970)
USGS COUNTY: Park County Sheet 1 of 4 (1975)

Bristlecone pines, the most durable organisms on this planet, are known to achieve lifespans of several thousand years. One specimen from Wheeler Peak in Humboldt National Forest, Nevada, has been dated by dendrochronology (counting of tree rings) at 4,900 years. The closest verified runner-up is the Sierra redwood of northern California, dated at 2,300 years. Native to the Rocky Mountains, bristlecones are found at elevations over 8,000 feet and are often at timberline.

Windy Ridge Bristlecone Pine Scenic Area, one of numerous stands of bristlecones in Colorado, was established by the Forest Service in 1964 at the eastern foot of Mount Bross, the 22nd-highest peak in the state at 14,172 feet. The winds, which give the ridge its name, cause the trees to take on a tilted appearance. This ridge offers good views of South Park. You may wish to estimate the age of the trees by counting the rings in the stumps of those trees unfortunately cut for mining timber.

DIRECTIONS: From the junction <0.0> of Colorado 9 and US 285 in Fairplay, follow Highway 9 north to the Alma city limit sign <5.7>. Continue past Park County 10, a side road <5.9> to the left. Turn left at an intersection <6.0> with a side road across from a gas station in the middle of Alma. Continue straight at the next intersection (one block from Colorado 9) and pass a blue sign <6.1> on the right (north) side of this good dirt road, identifying it as Park County 8. Continue on this road to a junction <8.8> with a road to the right marked as Forest Road 415 (access to Windy Ridge). Turn right and continue on this dirt road past Sawmill Creek <10.4> to where the road seems to empty into a mining area <11.8>. Bear left and wind uphill through the Mineral Park Mine remains. As the road curves to the right, ignore a side road <11.9> of questionable quality to the left labeled as Forest Road 857. Immediately thereafter, ford a small stream and continue up the hill on a slightly steeper portion of road. The road then curves to the left around some concrete foundations and then to the right as it climbs to the rim of Windy Ridge. A small parking area <12.4> is provided, or you can park back at the mining area and walk the last half mile.

The posture of bristlecone pines atop Windy Ridge illustrates the wind conditions.

*Courtesy of USDA Forest Service*

# 36 MOSQUITO PASS

TYPE: Mountain Scenery/Historic
ADMINISTRATION: Private land/Pike National Forest
QUALITY: Very scenic
ACCESS: Moderate 4WD
FACILITIES: None
TIME NEEDED: One hour
BEST VISIT: Midsummer to late summer
BEST PHOTO: Morning to midday
ELEVATION: 13,186 feet
REFERENCE: Fairplay
MAP: State highway map
San Isabel National Forest visitor map
USGS TOPO: Climax 7.5' (1970)
USGS COUNTY: Park County Sheet 1 of 4 (1975)
Lake County (1975)

Mosquito Pass, though not on the Continental Divide (the Divide is six miles north), is the highest through road in North America at 13,186 feet. It's an interesting trip, with a few steep grades, stretches of narrow shelf road, and impressive vistas. Leadville, for example, is visible over 3,000 feet below the pass in the Arkansas River Valley to the west. To the north is the head of this valley at Fremont Pass (on the Continental Divide), near Climax, site of a huge molybdenum mining operation. On a clear day, you can see mountains as far west as Mount Sopris and as far southeast as Pikes Peak. Many of Colorado's impressive peaks, including several "fourteeners," can be seen from here.

The search for gold first brought people to this area. In 1860, a mosquito was found pressed between the pages of a mining camp records book during a meeting. This insect became the namesake of the mining camp, the nearby creek, a whole mountain range, and the pass. Prospectors on foot and horseback used the pass, an old Indian trail, to cross from South Park to the goldfields of the Arkansas Valley. After the gold played out in 1867, there seemed little reason to use the pass. That was, of course, until someone discovered that the heavy black sand that always got in the way of gold mining was actually lead carbonate with a high silver content (hence the name Leadville). A boom of prosperity hit the valley.

This second discovery prompted the idea of building a wagon road over Mosquito Pass. The Mosquito Pass road would be half the length of the old Weston Pass route. October of 1878 saw the incorporation of the Mosquito Pass Wagon Road Company. Construction continued through the following unusually mild winter, and the road was opened in July 1879. The route received heavy use only until August 1880, when the railroad arrived in Leadville.

A stone marker, at the apex of the pass just north of the road, commemorates Methodist preacher John L. "Father" Dyer, the "Snowshoe Itinerant."

This old North London Mine boarding house was equipped with two additional entrances on the roof for access during deep winter storms.

This sign marks the summit of Mosquito Pass, which offers good views into the valleys both east and west.

# 36  MOSQUITO PASS

One of the first to conduct religious services in this mining district, Dyer supplemented his income by carrying mail over Mosquito Pass during the winter of 1863-64. He traveled using Norwegian snowshoes (homemade skis) that were about 10 feet in length. He usually crossed alone and at night, when the hard-frozen snow allowed him to make good time. The Dyer monument marks the high point of the annual Leadville Boom Days Pack Burro Race. Each participant must lead a burro loaded with a 33-pound miner's pack over a 23-mile course from the Lake County Courthouse in downtown Leadville, up Evans Gulch to the summit of Mosquito Pass, and down California Gulch to the finish line back at the Courthouse.

The mining district between Leadville and the pass makes finding the route difficult. For this reason, directions are given for following the pass road from east (Fairplay) to west (Leadville). This is a moderate four-wheel-drive road with a few rough spots just east of the pass and few places wide enough to pass approaching vehicles. Don't be misled because this road is shown on a highway map. It is not a passenger car route. Even if you don't have a rugged vehicle, it's worth the scenic trip from Fairplay up Mosquito Gulch as far as the first stagecoach-shaped sign at the base of the hill. From here, you may wish to walk to the North London Mine (1.2 miles). (All mines in the area are on private property.) It's also worthwhile exploring the mining district just east of Leadville. Tours are offered at Tabor's Matchless Mine.

**DIRECTIONS:** From the intersection <0.0> of Colorado 9 with US 285 in

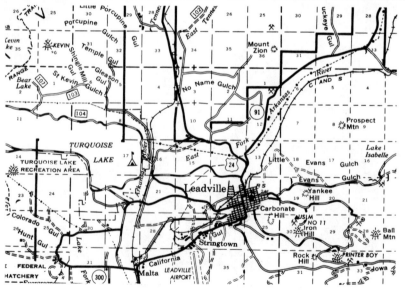

# 36   MOSQUITO PASS

**DIRECTIONS:** From the intersection <0.0> of Colorado 9 with US 285 in Fairplay, proceed north on Highway 9 toward Alma. Turn left (west) onto a side road <4.7> (Park County 12) marked by a sign identifying Mosquito Gulch. Follow this good dirt road, ignoring the side roads. Take the right fork (marked by a sign identifying Mosquito Pass) where the road splits <9.3>, with the left fork headed to the South London Mine. Keep left at a sign <11.7> identifying Mosquito Pass. Continue to a stagecoach-shaped sign <11.8> giving the history of the pass. Passenger cars should not go beyond this sign. More rugged vehicles can proceed up the hill. Keep left <12.8> to reach the North London Mine <13.0>. The mine is on private property, so please stay on the public road. Continue uphill, ignoring the side road <13.6> to the left. The road gets rough before reaching the summit <14.6>.

Leadville is reached by following this road west (downhill). Take the right fork, ignoring the road <15.2> on the left, and continue downhill. Stay on the road contained in the valley with several lakes; do not take the side road <16.1> that crosses the ridge to the right. As you enter the Leadville mining district, there are many side roads. Continue to go down and out (west). This rough road becomes a good dirt road <17.9> leading toward Leadville. Stay on the main road and continue past Tabor's Matchless Mine <20.9>. Pass a sign <21.4> (posted for eastbound traffic) marking this road as Lake County 3. Continue straight at an intersection <21.6> with Ash Street (you are now on 7th Street) and rejoin the pavement <21.7>. Pass a locomotive on display <21.9> and join US 24 in Leadville <22.1>.

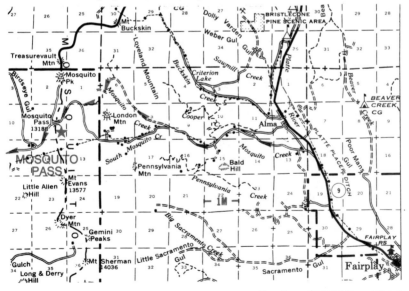

Courtesy of USDA Forest Service

# 37 CHALK CLIFFS

TYPE: Mountain Scenery/Geologic
ADMINISTRATION: San Isabel National Forest/Private land
QUALITY: Scenic
ACCESS: Paved road
FACILITIES: Nearby campgrounds
TIME NEEDED: Half hour
BEST VISIT: Spring to fall
BEST PHOTO: Morning to midday
ELEVATION: 10,034 feet (top of cliffs)
REFERENCE: Nathrop
MAP: State highway map
San Isabel National Forest visitor map
USGS TOPO: Poncha Springs 15' (1956)
USGS COUNTY: Chaffee County Sheet 2 of 3 (1980)

A section of steep, pure white cliffs, nearly 2,000 feet tall and 1.7 miles long, are at the southeastern base of Mount Princeton, Colorado's 18th highest peak at 14,197 feet. Mount Antero, ranking 10th highest at 14,269 feet, forms the south wall of Chalk Creek Valley. Both the creek and the cliffs are named for the formation's chalk-like appearance and coloration. Heated mineral waters follow subterranean faults inside Mount Princeton. These fluids have altered and leached feldspar in the Mount Princeton granite into kaolinite, the white substance forming the cliffs. Several hot springs emerge at Princeton Hot Springs near the eastern mouth of the valley.

There are tales of lost treasure here. Legend holds that early Spanish explorers raided an Indian camp at the base of the cliffs while the braves were away hunting. The intruders looted the village, removing several pieces of ornamental gold. When the returning village men discovered the theft, they pursued the marauders toward the Chalk Cliffs. The Spanish explorers supposedly stashed their plunder among the crevices of the cliffs before the Indians killed most of the group and drove off the rest. It is said that more than one contemporary treasure hunter has fallen to his death while searching for this lost loot.

DIRECTIONS: Follow Colorado 162 west from its junction <0.0> with US 285 in Nathrop. This intersection is marked with a green sign identifying access for Mount Princeton and Saint Elmo. Continue on this paved road (offering fine views of Mounts Princeton and Antero) past a San Isabel National Forest sign <4.0>. Colorado 162 becomes Chaffee County 162 <4.6> and continues up the valley. Go straight where Chaffee County 290 <5.7> splits off to the left. Pull over to the side of the road <6.0> for good views of Chalk Cliffs to the north (right). Please enjoy the scenery from the road because a strip of private land separates you from the cliffs.

Chalk Cliffs, white as snow, stand at the base of 14,197-foot Mount Princeton.

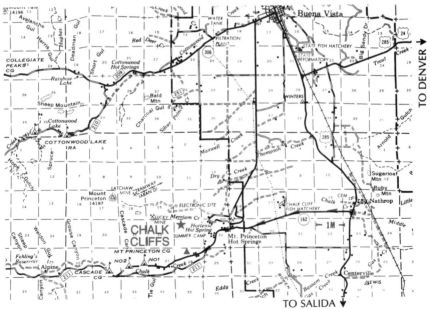

Courtesy of USDA Forest Service

# 38   SAINT ELMO

TYPE: Mountain Scenery/Historic
ADMINISTRATION: Private land
QUALITY: Scenic
ACCESS: Good dirt road
FACILITIES: General store/Rest rooms
TIME NEEDED: One hour
BEST VISIT: Early summer to fall
BEST PHOTO: Morning to afternoon
ELEVATION: 10,000 feet
REFERENCE: Saint Elmo
MAP: State highway map
San Isabel National Forest visitor map
USGS TOPO: Garfield 15' (1940)
USGS COUNTY: Chaffee County Sheet 2 of 3 (1980)

Saint Elmo, in Chalk Creek Valley, was formally laid out in October 1880. The town's original population of less than 500 named it Forest City. This made sense, as the entire valley floor was covered by dense stands of evergreens. To avoid confusion with a town of the same name in California, the US Post Office asked that the name of this new town be changed. The residents obliged by adopting the new name of Saint Elmo. The town's population peaked in 1882 at approximately 2,000. It had several hotels (including the large Clifton Hotel), a post office, a newspaper, many businesses and stores, a town hall, a school, and the usual saloons. The town never had a church, even though the town hall with its bell steeple resembles one. Religious services were held by Father Dyer (see site 36) and Bishop Macheboeuf whenever either was in town and could find a place to gather a group. After the schoolhouse was completed in 1882, services were held there.

Mining was St. Elmo's primary reason for existence. The Mary Murphy mine, established in 1875, was the largest producer in the district and continued to operate into the 1920s. Ores worth more than 14 million dollars were extracted from this mine. In its peak year of 1914, the Mary Murphy employed over 250 miners. A mile-long tram transported ore down the mountain slopes to the railroad grade in the valley. You can still see some of this equipment a few miles south of town. Many other mines, including the Iron Chest, Tilden Campaign, and Pioneer, also worked the district's gold, silver, and less valuable metal ores. After the boom decades of the 1880s and '90s, both mining and the town declined.

Mining was not the only reason for the town, however. Saint Elmo was also the principal supply center for the Denver, South Park, and Pacific Railroad, which was constructing the Alpine Tunnel during 1880 and 1881. The story of the Alpine Tunnel is a fascinating chapter in Colorado's historic railroad era. The 1,771-foot long tunnel at 11,523 feet was bored under the Continental Divide in just 18 months. The work, continuing even in winter,

STATE OF COLORADO

Saint Elmo is one of Colorado's most accessible ghost towns.

Careful inspection reveals the words "Miners Exchange" on the false front of the building on the right.

was so demanding that most men stayed on the job only a few weeks. The tunnel supported a construction crew of only 400 at a time, despite a turnover in the labor force of more than 10,000 men. When the line was completed to Gunnison, Saint Elmo became an important stop for freight and passenger trains. Saint Elmo was also an important terminal for stage and freight traffic over Tincup Pass. This pass, northwest of Saint Elmo on the Continental Divide, was an important early crossing to Tincup and Taylor Park beyond. This route is now a rugged jeep road.

With all the mining, railroad, and wagon freight activity, Saint Elmo was a bustling town. On Saturday nights, miners and railroad men gathered in town. Most of the town survived the fire of 1890 that destroyed two blocks, but it could not survive the loss of railroad service in 1926 because of the decline of mining. Saint Elmo soon became a ghost town. Many of the original buildings still stand. The town hall, general store, and many of the old false-fronted businesses continue to line the main street. The school is on the north side of town (as are the public rest rooms). All of the buildings in

# 38 SAINT ELMO

town are privately owned, so please respect the rights of these property holders. Passenger cars can follow the old railroad grade south out of town as far as the site of Hancock. From there, you can walk to the east portal of the Alpine Tunnel or jeep across Hancock Pass to join the western grade of the railroad as it descends toward Quartz Creek.

**DIRECTIONS:** Follow Colorado 162 west from its junction <0.0> with US 285 in Nathrop, just south of Buena Vista. Ignore the many side roads and stay on paved Colorado 162, which later becomes Chaffee County 162 (a good graveled road also known as Forest Route 211), continuing all the way to Saint Elmo. You will pass the Chalk Cliffs <6.0> (see site 37), Mount Princeton Campground <8.4>, Chalk Lake Campground <8.9>, Cascade Campground <9.6>, and side roads to Alpine townsite <12.3>, Mount Antero <12.4>, Hancock townsite <15.6>, and Iron City Campground <15.7>. Saint Elmo <15.8> is marked by a sign asking visitors to please respect the rights of the private property owners.

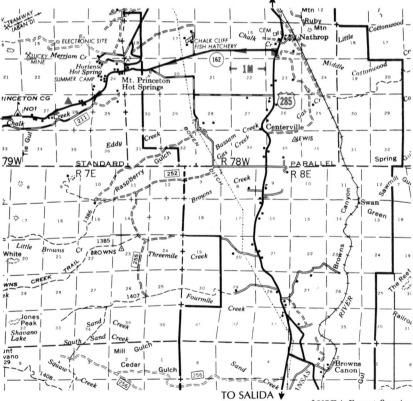

TO SALIDA ▼

*Courtesy of USDA Forest Service*

# 39  MONARCH PASS

**TYPE:** Mountain Scenery
**ADMINISTRATION:** San Isabel and Gunnison National Forests
**QUALITY:** Scenic
**ACCESS:** Paved road
**FACILITIES:** Visitor Center
**TIME NEEDED:** Half hour
**BEST VISIT:** Early summer to fall
**BEST PHOTO:** Afternoon
**ELEVATION:** 11,312 feet
**REFERENCE:** Poncha Springs
**MAP:** State highway map
**USGS TOPO:** Pahlone Peak 7.5′ (1967), Garfield 15′ (1940)
**USGS COUNTY:** Chaffee County Sheet 3 of 3 (1980)
Gunnison County Sheet 5 of 6 (1976)

From the summit of Monarch Pass astride the Continental Divide, there are pleasant vistas into the surrounding Sawatch Range, especially to the north and east. A small National Forest Visitor Center at the southeastern edge of the parking area displays some of the local wildlife, including the bobcat, stellar jay, red-tailed hawk, white-tailed ptarmigan, pika, and porcupine. A separate display shows several Rocky Mountain wildflowers including kingscrown, dwarf clover, alpine primrose, monkeyflower, and pinnate leaf daisy. A satellite photo of the region taken from 500 miles above the earth shows the rugged terrain along this part of the Continental Divide.

A narrative on the Divide explains that it is the separation line between drainages reaching either the Atlantic or Pacific oceans. The Divide stretches over 2,000 miles from Alaska to Mexico and is the source of many of America's major rivers. In Colorado, the Arkansas, Rio Grande, and Platte rivers originate along the Divide and flow eastward toward the Atlantic. The Colorado River drains all of the western slope water toward the Pacific Ocean. Most of the peaks along the Divide vary from 12,000 to 14,000 feet. The highest point on the Divide itself is 14,270 feet at the summit of Grays Peak (85 miles northeast of Monarch Pass). Other displays include history, recreation, and mining narratives. The history of local railroads, responsible for much of the region's mining growth, is also given in the Visitor Center.

Monarch Pass is Colorado's third-highest all-weather pass. The original wagon road of the 1880s was graded and and graveled in 1922, becoming the first automobile crossing of the pass. The modern highway, completed in 1939, reroutes traffic over a new crossing slightly southeast of Old Monarch Pass. The name "Monarch" comes from a mine on the eastern slope of the pass. A large limestone quarry near Monarch Mine was operated by Colorado Fuel and Iron to obtain flux for its steel mills in Pueblo.

**DIRECTIONS:** Monarch Pass, on US 50, is 17.5 miles west of the westernmost junction of US 50 and US 285 in Poncha Springs, just west of Salida.

Monarch Pass offers impressive views into the surrounding Sawatch Range.

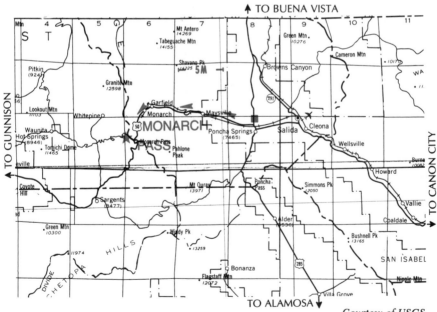

*Courtesy of USGS*

# COLORADO SPRINGS DISTRICT

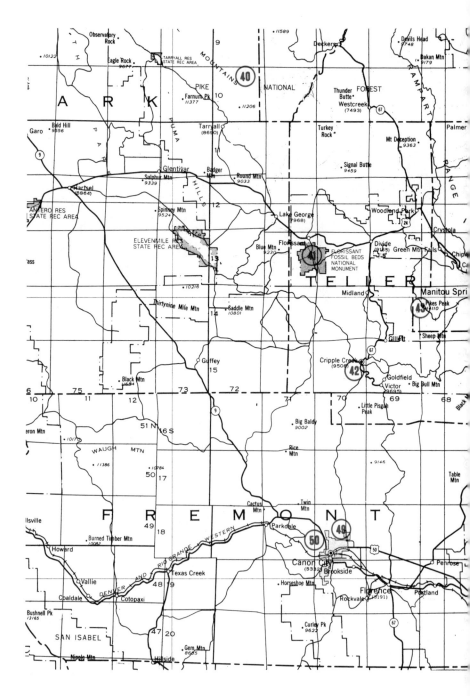

# COLORADO SPRINGS DISTRICT

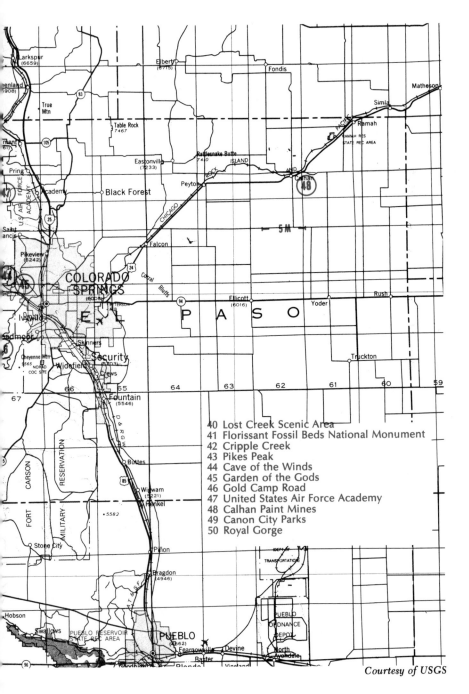

40 Lost Creek Scenic Area
41 Florissant Fossil Beds National Monument
42 Cripple Creek
43 Pikes Peak
44 Cave of the Winds
45 Garden of the Gods
46 Gold Camp Road
47 United States Air Force Academy
48 Calhan Paint Mines
49 Canon City Parks
50 Royal Gorge

*Courtesy of USGS*

# 40 LOST CREEK SCENIC AREA

TYPE: Mountain Scenery/Geologic
ADMINISTRATION: Pike National Forest
QUALITY: Scenic
ACCESS: Good dirt road and hike
FACILITIES: Nearby campgrounds
TIME NEEDED: One day
BEST VISIT: Early summer to fall
BEST PHOTO: Morning to midday
ELEVATION: 8,730 feet (between Lost and Goose Creeks)
REFERENCE: Deckers
MAP: Pike National Forest visitor map
USGS TOPO: Cheesman Lake 7.5' (1978)
McCurdy Mountain 7.5' (1956)
USGS COUNTY: Jefferson County Sheet 2 of 2 (1976)
Park County Sheet 2 of 4 (1976)

Lost Creek Scenic Area, within Lost Creek Wilderness, covers approximately 27 square miles of Pike National Forest. The parallel ridges of the Tarryall and Kenosha mountains form a valley that holds Lost Creek. East is the Rampart Range running between Denver and Colorado Springs. The higher surrounding peaks reach an altitude of 11,000 to 12,000 feet, and most of the trails follow creeks at 8,000 to 9,000 feet. Because this vicinity is lower than much of Colorado's sky-scraping mountain topography, it offers a different kind of scenery and allows visits much earlier in the year. The area is heavily forested and dissected by a network of streams. Though its rock formations are not dramatic, they are numerous, pleasant to study, and fun to explore. The rock of these formations and the surrounding summits is Pikes Peak granite, characteristically reddish in color, of coarse construction, and lacking in durability, making it an easy target for erosion. The entire area is littered with rounded rock fragments from pebble- to house-sized. (Weathering works on the sharp points and edges first, leaving rounded shapes.) Stacks, piles, and jumbles of these rocks have filled the valley bottoms, providing the area's many scenic formations.

So extensive is this matrix of rubble that many streams disappear into crevices at various places. Lost Creek received its name because it vanishes for several long stretches. Near the middle of the Scenic Area, Lost Creek disappears under a sizable hill of broken rock. Many observers have been confused as to the source of this "new" stream—called Goose Creek—where Lost Creek emerges from under the hill.

These formations also contain numerous caves or shafts; they may be dangerous and require spelunking equipment and safety precautions even for partial exploration. These may be the longest rubble caves in America. There are at least 11 tunnels, some suspected of being longer than 2,000 feet. One of these tunnels near the Shafthouse, site of a failed attempt to dam a subterranean creek, is a source of year-round ice.

Lost Creek combines the scenery of forest, stream, and unusual rock formations.

Many of the area's granite boulders have been eroded into rounded art forms.

# 40 LOST CREEK SCENIC AREA

Lost Creek Scenic Area provides a fine opportunity for day hikes and overnight backpacking trips. It is a good balance between vegetation, mountain scenery, and numerous sources of water. If you're lucky, you may also catch a glimpse of the Rocky Mountain bighorn sheep that are occasionally seen in the vicinity.

**DIRECTIONS:** From Colorado Springs, proceed west on US 24 to its junction <0.0> with Colorado 67 North in Woodland Park. Follow Colorado 67 to Deckers <23.1>, where the road encounters a multiple fork. Continue straight on the paved road across a bridge into Jefferson County (County Road 126). Continue past Lone Rock Campground <23.7> and

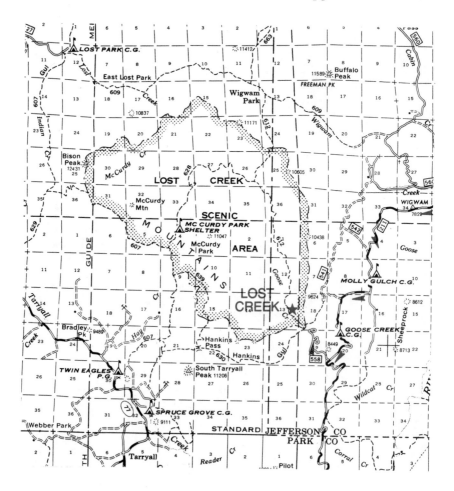

turn left onto a signed dirt road <25.8>. This road starts out narrow but later widens into a good dirt road. Turn right onto a side road <27.9> and pass a small radio tower <28.5> on the left. Continue to a fork <29.0> marked by a brown sign. Take the left fork toward Goose Creek Campground. Continue past Molley Gulch Campground <34.1> to a fork <34.3>. Take the road on the right toward Goose Creek Campground. Continue past Goose Creek Campground <37.3> (rest rooms) to a side road <39.1> on the right marked by a brown sign as the entrance road to Lost Creek Scenic Area. Take this short entrance road to the parking area <40.4>. A sign marks the trailhead just southwest of the parking lot.

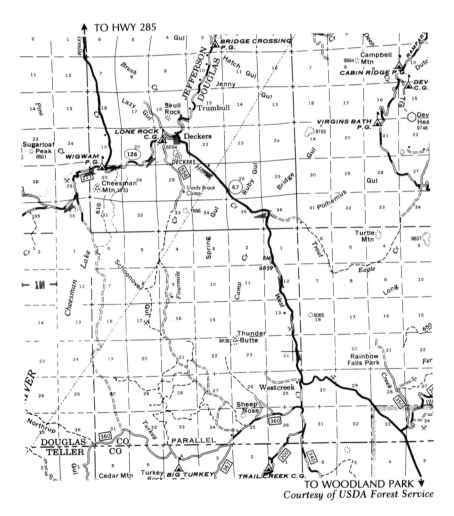

TO WOODLAND PARK ▼

*Courtesy of USDA Forest Service*

# 41  FLORISSANT FOSSIL BEDS

TYPE: Mountain Scenery/Paleontologic
ADMINISTRATION: National Monument
QUALITY: Scenic
ACCESS: Good dirt road
FACILITIES: Visitor Center/Picnic area
TIME NEEDED: Half day
BEST VISIT: Spring to fall
BEST PHOTO: Morning
ELEVATION: 8,320 feet (Visitor Center)
REFERENCE: Florissant
MAP: State highway map
Pike National Forest visitor map
USGS TOPO: Lake George 7.5' (1975)
USGS COUNTY: Teller County (1980)

Florissant Fossil Beds National Monument is the home of some of the world's largest petrified tree stumps and some of the most delicate fossilized insects ever discovered. The fossils resulted from volvcanic activity during Oligocene times (approximately 35 million years ago) from the Thirtynine Mile volcanic field near Guffey, 15 miles southwest of the monument. Mud and lava flows blocked several streams, forming a shallow lake where the monument is now located. This irregularly shaped lake, subsequently named Lake Florissant, received numerous volcanic ash showers from the nearby volcanic field over half a million years. The combination of fine-grained ash and lake waters made an environment conducive to fossil formation. Thousands of insects and small animals were trapped by the ash falls and were carried to the lake bottom. The deposited ash made a thin-layered shale, sometimes known as paper shale, containing the numerous fossils. These bottom layers have yielded the most intricate fossils. Insects as tiny as mosquitos were preserved in minute detail.

The fossil beds were first described by Dr. A. C. Peale during the Hayden geological survey of 1874. Since then, many scientists have come to Florissant seeking rare insect specimens. Over 80,000 fossils have been removed. Specimens of small mammals, birds, and fish have also been discovered. Over 140 species of leaves and whole plants were also preserved here. More than 1,100 insect species have been identified, including almost all of the known New World butterfly fossils.

Several petrified tree stumps have been excavated for view. The larger of these are remains of sequoias, similar to the redwoods that inhabit the present California coast. These stumps are among the largest petrified trees in the world. Big Stump, which measures 13 feet in diameter, stands 10 feet tall and weighs around 140 tons in its present condition. This tree likely stood 300 feet tall and was probably 700 to 1,500 years old when it and the surrounding trees were buried to a depth of 14 feet by ash and mud. Another interesting stump, the Trio, is a group of three sequoias with intermingled

The Trio is a group of petrified sequoia stumps near the Visitor Center of Florissant Fossil Beds National Monument.

# 41 FLORISSANT FOSSIL BEDS

roots. Each of the three stumps is 19 feet in circumference and attains a height of 14 feet. A metal cable binds each stump to prevent fragmentation. Most of these stumps, which were uncovered in the 1920s as part of a commercial attraction, are splintering and weathering from exposure to temperature changes and the elements.

The monument contains a Visitor Center with a nearby picnic area. Overnight accommodations should be sought outside the monument because it closes at night. The Visitor Center contains a small museum that displays many fossil specimens. A magnifying glass (provided) is needed to study the fine detail of some of the smaller items. The Trio is immediately west of the Visitor Center on a nature trail that passes several other excavated stumps. Big Stump is half a mile north of the Visitor Center near another group of petrified stumps. There are more than a dozen large stumps on display within the monument. Please do not disturb or remove any fossil specimens.

**DIRECTIONS:** The town of Florissant is 35 miles west of Colorado Springs on US 24. In the center of this small town, a dirt road leaves to the south and is marked by a green sign identifying this as the turn for Florissant Fossil Beds National Monument. Turn south onto this good dirt road <0.0> and continue to a junction <2.3> with a side road to the right (west). Turn right onto this road to reach the Visitor Center.

This wasp is an example of the fine preservation of detail found in thousands of insect fossils unearthed at Florissant.

# 41 FLORISSANT FOSSIL BEDS

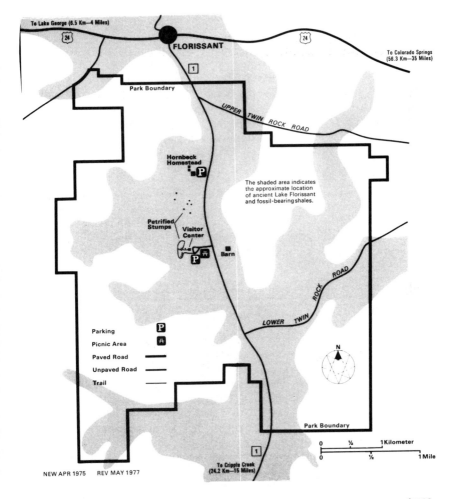

To Lake George (6.5 Km—4 Miles)

24

FLORISSANT

24

To Colorado Springs
(56.3 Km—35 Miles)

1

Park Boundary

UPPER TWIN ROCK ROAD

Hornbeck
Homestead

P

The shaded area indicates
the approximate location
of ancient Lake Florissant
and fossil-bearing shales.

Petrified
Stumps

Visitor
Center

P

Barn

ROCK ROAD

LOWER TWIN

Parking          P

Picnic Area      🛆

Paved Road       ▬

Unpaved Road     ▬

Trail            ▬

N

Park Boundary

0        ½        1 Kilometer
0        ½        1 Mile

1

To Cripple Creek
(24.2 Km—15 Miles)

NEW APR 1975     REV MAY 1977

*Courtesy of NPS*

# 42   CRIPPLE CREEK

TYPE: Mountain Scenery/Historic
ADMINISTRATION: Private land
QUALITY: Scenic
ACCESS: Paved road
FACILITIES: Commercial attractions
TIME NEEDED: Half day
BEST VISIT: Spring to fall
BEST PHOTO: Midday
ELEVATION: 9,508 feet
REFERENCE: Cripple Creek
MAP: State highway map
Pike National Forest visitor map
USGS TOPO: South Cripple Creek 7.5' (1975)
North Cripple Creek 7.5' (1975)
USGS COUNTY: Teller County (1980)

The Cripple Creek area and other sites in the Pikes Peak region were prospected in the early 1860s as part of Colorado's fledgling gold rush. The district showed little promise, however. In the mid-1870s, a few deposits were unearthed on Mount Pisgah, but the meager yield led to a short-lived boom. Stories of a strike in 1884 started another local rush. Claims were quickly sold for exorbitant amounts until miners discovered that Mount McIntyre had been "salted." After these mining failures, most considered the area to be of no mineral interest. The unlikely terrain was more typical of ranch land than of mineral belts. The area soon reverted to its apparent potential, grazing land.

Bob Womack, a local cowpoke, divided his time between herding cattle for the neighboring ranchers and digging small prospect holes all over the landscape. The local ranchers called him a dreamer to still be prospecting in this unproductive district. Furthermore, they didn't appreciate all those holes, into which cattle might fall. One day in late 1890, samples that Womack excavated from Poverty Gulch were assayed in Colorado Springs and showed rich gold ore. Word soon got out, and many prospectors began to appear in the area. Cripple Creek was destined to become Colorado's last great gold camp.

Several mining towns quickly sprang up at the bases of the many low hills characteristic of the district. Two of these towns were Fremont and Hayden Placer, adjacent rivals until they were consolidated under the name Cripple Creek in 1893. The name reportedly comes from a cow having stumbled and crippled its leg in a local creek. Two Denver real estate developers were quick to lay out a town plan and sell lots. They also loaned their names to the town's two main streets, Bennett and Myers avenues. Bennett Avenue became the center of respectable business activity, while Myers Avenue became home to gambling houses, saloons, and parlor houses. The popula-

Cripple Creek, still very much inhabited, has a thriving tourist business in addition to recently revived mining activity in the district.

Numerous mining relics are scattered along the hillsides between the towns of Cripple Creek and Victor.

# 42 CRIPPLE CREEK

tion of the town peaked at the turn of the century. Some estimates go as high as 100,000 residents, but a third of this amount is more likely.

Cripple Creek was a major boom town. It was served by three different railroads plus two local electric streetcar lines that connected the district's camps. At one time, 58 trains each day reached the stations of Cripple Creek. The narrow-gauge Florence and Cripple Creek Railroad was the first to reach the town in 1894 by way of Phantom Canyon, which ran south to the Arkansas River near Canon City. Eighteen months later, the standard-gauge Midland Terminal connected the town with Colorado Springs by crossing Ute Pass to Divide, where it then headed south toward the district. The final line to reach Cripple Creek was not finished until five years later. The Colorado Springs and Cripple Creek District Railroad, a standard-gauge route better known as the "Short Line," reached town in 1901. This was the shortest (45 miles) and most scenic access to the district, and it became a major tourist attraction in its own right (see site 46). All three routes are now passenger car roads.

The search for gold was different here than in other mining districts in Colorado. Experienced prospectors didn't have the usual signs of quartz veins in exposed rock to guide them. Mines were located simply by guessing; the very lucky struck it rich. More than a score of millionaires were produced by the buried wealth. Well over 100 million dollars in gold has been extracted from the district. Mines are everywhere: practically every rock on every square mile of hillside was turned over in search of the precious ore. The Portland mine, largest in the district with shafts descending 3,000 feet, employed over 700 men (including, at one time, Jack Dempsey) and produced over 60 million dollars in ore. This boom, unlike others in Colorado's history, lasted well into the twentieth century.

Today, Cripple Creek offers many attractions and services for the visitor: mine tours, renovated buildings, shops, museums, and a narrow-gauge train ride from Cripple Creek toward Victor. Victorian melodramas are staged at the restored Imperial Hotel, which draws thousands of spectators each year. You may also notice that some of the district's mines have recently been reactivated because of the present high value of gold ore. Be sure to drive the paved road that connects Cripple Creek with Victor (home of Lowell Thomas) to the south. The view of Battle Mountain, north of Victor, is staggering; the hillside is almost completely covered by mining ruins.

**DIRECTIONS:** From Colorado Springs, proceed west on US 24 to its junction with Colorado Highway 67 South in Divide (not Colorado 67 North in Woodland Park). Turn left at this intersection <0.0> and follow Colorado 67 south to the town of Cripple Creek. You will pass through an old railroad tunnel <9.2> and by the Mollie Kathleen Mine <16.8> (tours) to reach Cripple Creek <18.4>. For the best mining scenery, continue south on Colorado 67 to Victor <24.5> and just beyond on the paved road to a sign <25.1> giving the history of Battle Mountain.

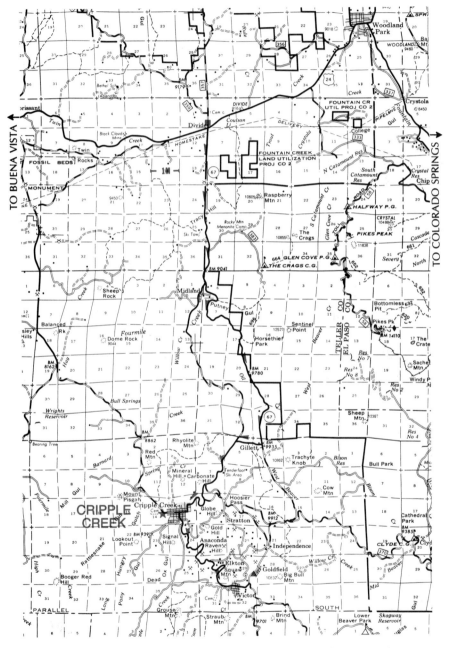

*Courtesy of USDA Forest Service*

# 43  PIKES PEAK

TYPE: Mountain Scenery/Historic
ADMINISTRATION: Pike National Forest
QUALITY: Scenic
ACCESS: Good dirt road
FACILITIES: Summit house/Picnic areas
TIME NEEDED: Half day
BEST VISIT: Midsummer to late summer
BEST PHOTO: Morning
ELEVATION: 14,110 feet (summit)
REFERENCE: Colorado Springs
MAP: State highway, Pike National Forest visitor map
USGS TOPO: Pikes Peak 7.5' (1976),Woodland Park 7.5' (1976)
USGS COUNTY: El Paso County Sheet 1 of 4 (1978)
Teller County (1980)

Pikes Peak is perhaps the best known of all of America's mountains and receives more visitation than any other peak in the country. It is not the highest mountain in Colorado (it ranks 28th), but with no neighboring "fourteeners," the mountain, with its characteristic reddish granite composition, takes on singularly dramatic proportions, especially when viewed from Colorado's eastern plains. Pikes Peak rises more than 7,000 feet above the surrounding terrain, a larger elevation difference than anywhere else in the state.

The mountain first became known from the reports of Captain Zebulon Montgomery Pike, who was sent to map the southwestern boundary of the Louisiana Purchase. Pike and a group of three climbers attempted to scale the mountain on November 24, 1806, but were driven back by the winter weather. Pike concluded that this "Highest Peak" could never be climbed under these conditions. Dr. Edwin James of the Long Expedition achieved the first recorded ascent of Pikes Peak on July 14, 1820.

The US Army built a small stone weather station at the summit in 1873. It was staffed year-round until 1889, and one of the observers received national attention from his totally erroneous stories of giant mountain rats devouring small children near the summit. The first carriage road to the top was built in 1889 and was heavily used until completion of the cog railway a year later. Construction of the present automobile road began in 1915. The lack of maintenance during a later period seemed to doom the road for abandonment until the city of Colorado Springs agreed to operate it as a toll road, using the receipts to maintain it. An alternative way to the summit is the scenic cog railway from Manitou Springs. When you see the view from the top, you will understand why Katharine Lee Bates was inspired to write "America the Beautiful" after her visit here in 1893.

DIRECTIONS: From the junction <0.0> of US 24 and Interstate 25 in Colorado Springs, proceed west on US 24 to Cascade, where a large sign marks the turn <11.5> for the toll road. Beyond the toll gate <12.7>, a good dirt road covers the additional 19 miles to the summit.

# 43 PIKES PEAK

*Pikes Peak, framed by the Gateway Rocks of Garden of the Gods, stands as lone sentinel above this region of Colorado.*

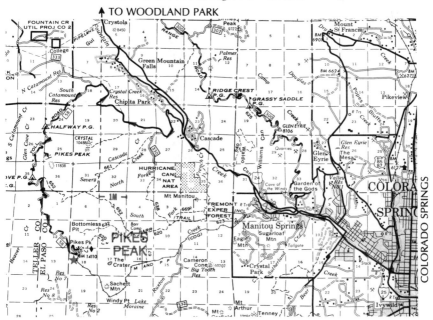

*Courtesy of USDA Forest Service*

# 44 CAVE OF THE WINDS

**TYPE:** Geologic Scenery
**ADMINISTRATION:** Private land
**QUALITY:** Scenic
**ACCESS:** Paved road
**FACILITIES:** Commercial attraction
**TIME NEEDED:** Two hours
**BEST VISIT:** All year
**BEST PHOTO:** Midday (Williams Canyon)
**ELEVATION:** 7,020 feet (entry building)
**REFERENCE:** Colorado Springs
**MAP:** State highway, Pike National Forest visitor map
**USGS TOPO:** Manitou Springs 7.5' (1975)
**USGS COUNTY:** El Paso County Sheet 1 of 4 (1978)

There is considerable confusion as to the modern discoverer of Cave of the Winds and Manitou Grand Caverns. William Kimberly was the first to spread a rumor of the existence of Manitou Grand Caverns among the inhabitants of Colorado Springs. He reportedly stumbled upon the entrance while in a drunken stupor in 1862. The first on record to refer to Cave of the Winds was Arthur Love, who, with his brothers, homesteaded in Williams Canyon in 1870. He cleared a path to the cave entrance and purchased the parcel of land containing the cave. It was not until George Snider took an interest in the cave, however, that its commercial potential was fully appreciated. During 1879 and 1880, Snider explored most of the passageways and rooms of Cave of the Winds and in 1881 acquired the property and opened the cave for an entry fee of $1.00. In the early 1900s, a connecting passageway was bored between Manitou Grand Caverns and Cave of the Winds, and the consolidated attraction kept the name Cave of the Winds.

The cave passageways total just under a mile, making it the fifth largest cave in Colorado. The cave is formed from the lower layers of Leadville limestone and the upper strata of Manitou dolomite. The system spans about 250 vertical feet of these layers. Cave of the Winds contains many fine examples of limestone speleothems (cave formations), including some that are quite rare.

Guided tours through 20 rooms of formations take about 40 minutes and begin every 15 minutes. Comfortable walking shoes and a light jacket are recommended. For the more adventurous, the "Wild Tour" of Manitou Grand Caverns offers a half-day trip through the noncommercial part of the cave. Old clothes, a flashlight, and at least 24-hour advance reservations (303/658-5397) are required.

**DIRECTIONS:** From the junction <0.0> of US 24 and Interstate 25 (exit 141) in Colorado Springs, proceed west on US 24 to a junction <5.5> with a paved road to the right. This exit is well marked by a green sign as Cave of the Winds Road. Turn right and follow this road uphill to the parking lot.

The interior of Cave of the Winds offers many interesting speleothems.

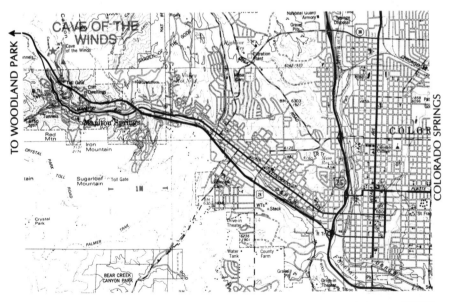

*Courtesy of USGS*

# 45 GARDEN OF THE GODS

**TYPE:** Foothills Scenery/Geologic
**ADMINISTRATION:** Public land—Colorado Springs City Park
**QUALITY:** Extremely scenic
**ACCESS:** Paved road
**FACILITIES:** Visitor Center/Picnic areas
**TIME NEEDED:** Half day
**BEST VISIT:** Spring to fall
**BEST PHOTO:** Early morning to late afternoon
**ELEVATION:** 6,405 feet (base of Gateway Rocks)
**REFERENCE:** Colorado Springs
**MAP:** Pike National Forest visitor map
**USGS TOPO:** Cascade 7.5' (1969)
Manitou Springs 7.5' (1975)
Pikeview 7.5' (1975)
**USGS COUNTY:** El Paso County Sheet 1 of 4 (1978)

Garden of the Gods is part of the hogbacks that typify the meeting of mountains and plains along many miles of the Front and Rampart ranges of the Rocky Mountains. The many horizontal layers of sediment making Colorado's eastern plains have been tilted and warped by the rise of the present Rockies. This rearrangement of sedimentary strata has reached a scenic zenith at Garden of the Gods. Some of these layers stand vertically; others have been eroded into fascinating, streamlined sculptures. Gypsum, shale, conglomerate, and sandstone of various colors can all be found in the park.

Balanced Rock, composed largely of erosion-resistant conglomerate, rests precariously on a layer of shale that is nearly weathered away. West of Balanced Rock, in an area known as Mushroom Park, other towers and pedestals similar to Balanced Rock were formed. These deep red layers of conglomerate and shale are only slightly tilted; they are separated by a fault from the nearly vertical layers in the park's eastern section. These tall slabs are composed of white and salmon-colored sandstone, with an exposure of gypsum visible nearby. At one time, other material touched these layers as they were shifted into a perpendicular attitude. The less erosion-resistant substances have since weathered away, leaving the tough, vertical layers standing in isolation.

The Utes and numerous plains tribes of the region were aware of Garden of the Gods long before American explorers arrived. The expedition group of Major Stephen Long sighted Garden of the Gods in 1820, and from his party made the first recorded ascent of Pikes Peak to the southwest. Colorado City (now in the western part of Colorado Springs) was founded by Colonel Melancthon F. Beach and Rufus E. Cable in 1859, the year Colorado's gold rush began. These two men are credited with naming the park. It is said that Colonel Beach suggested the area would make a great beer garden. Mr. Cable then retorted that the location was better fit as a garden of the gods.

Balanced Rock is perhaps the most famous, though not the largest, of the world's balanced formations.

# 45  GARDEN OF THE GODS

Despite the encroachment of white settlers, the local Indian tribes, including a band of over 1,000 Utes who wintered just south of Balanced Rock during the winter of 1866-67, continued to use the area as late as 1878. Colorado Springs was established in 1871 by General William Jackson Palmer, founder of the Denver and Rio Grande Railroad. Charles E. Perkins, president of the Burlington Railroad, purchased 240 acres of Garden of the Gods in 1879. In 1886, Congress rejected a proposal to create a national park from 30 square miles of land including Pikes Peak and Garden of the Gods. Garden of the Gods was deeded to the city of Colorado Springs in 1909 by the family of Charles Perkins, with the stipulation that the site remain open to the public and free of charge for all time. In 1915, the city built the Hidden Inn immediately west of the North Gateway Rock, where it continues to cater to visiting tourists. A tradition began in 1921 when Rev. Albert Luce held the first Easter sunrise service in Garden of the Gods.

Balanced Rock was not included in the land originally given to the city, and it was not until 1932 that Colorado Springs acquired it and 275 acres of surrounding land from Paul Goerke. In prior years, Balanced Rock had been fenced by tall planks to block the view, and an admission charge was collected from the many who wished to view this famous formation. During the mid-1930s, trails and other developments were completed by the Civilian Conservation Corps, and chuckwagon dinners were first served by the Junior Chamber of Commerce. In the following years, several small segments of land were added to the park. In 1971, Garden of the Gods was designated a Registered Natural Landmark by the federal government.

Today, the park contains a network of roads and walking paths allowing visitors to easily reach most of the interesting rock formations. The best-known are Balanced Rock in the southwest portion of the park and the Gateway Rocks that stand as a set of 300-foot tall vertical walls at the northeastern edge. Be sure to look for the Kissing Camels atop the North Gateway Rock. A Visitor Center offers information on the geologic history as well as assistance in locating the formations. Picnic areas are located throughout the park.

**DIRECTIONS:** To enter Garden of the Gods by the Gateway Rocks entrance, take exit 146 off Interstate 25 in Colorado Springs for Garden of the Gods Road. From this exit <0.0>, proceed west to a T-intersection <2.4> where a sign indicates a left turn for Garden of the Gods. Turn left and, shortly thereafter, take the right fork <3.0> that goes downhill. Turn right at a junction <3.8> with a paved road marked by a sign identifying the entrance to Garden of the Gods.

To enter Garden of the Gods by the Balanced Rock entrance, proceed west on US 24 from its junction <0.0> with exit 141 on Interstate 25. Exit at Manitou Avenue <4.0> identified by a sign as the exit for Garden of the Gods. Follow the signs as they direct you to make several quick turns to reach the south entrance road to the park.

Gateway Rocks form the portal of the north entrance to Garden of the Gods.

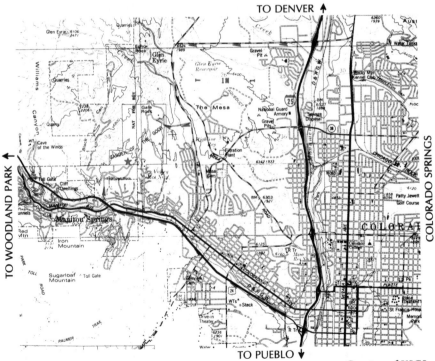

*Courtesy of USGS*

# 46 GOLD CAMP ROAD

TYPE: Mountain Scenery/Historic
ADMINISTRATION: Pike National Forest/Private land
QUALITY: Very scenic
ACCESS: Good dirt road
FACILITIES: Campgrounds
TIME NEEDED: Half day
BEST VISIT: Early summer to fall
BEST PHOTO: Morning to midday
ELEVATION: 7,480 feet (North Cheyenne Canyon road)
REFERENCE: Colorado Springs
MAP: State highway map
Pike National Forest visitor map
USGS TOPO: Manitou Springs 7.5' (1975)
Mount Big Chief 7.5' (1975)
Big Bull Mountain 7.5' (1975)
USGS COUNTY: El Paso County Sheet 1 of 4 (1978)
El Paso County Sheet 3 of 4 (1978)
Teller County (1980)

Gold Camp Road, an auto route, is the converted grade of the Colorado Springs and Cripple Creek District Railway, better known as the "Short Line." This was one of three railroads serving Cripple Creek when it was the world's greatest gold camp (see site 42). Colorado Springs banker Irving Howbert started the line in cooperation with local townspeople who owned mining interests in the Cripple Creek district. This standard-gauge line, completed in 1901, was sometimes called the "gold-plated railroad" because it had the best equipment available. The route became a major attraction in its own right because of its magnificent scenery. After making this journey, President Theodore Roosevelt called it the trip that "bankrupts the English language." The last train ran in 1920 because of the decline of mining at Cripple Creek. The railroad was bought by W. D. Corley, a Colorado Springs businessman, who converted it to a toll road. It became a public road in 1936. This road is not suitable for wide or long vehicles. Drivers should exercise caution while passing through one-lane rock cuts and tunnels.

DIRECTIONS: In Colorado Springs, proceed 2.1 miles west on US 24 from its interchange with Interstate 25 (exit 141). Turn left onto 26th Street <0.0>, marked by a sign for Gold Camp Road. Continue straight on this road; ignore the side roads. Turn right at an intersection <1.5> with a graveled road labeled by a small green sign as Gold Camp Road. You are now on the old railroad grade. Ignore an intersection <2.5> and continue on the paved road that climbs the outside of the hill. Again, stay on the main road and ignore the side roads. A turnout <4.5> yields good views of Colorado Springs below. The pavement ends <4.9> just before you

Cathedral Park is one of the most inspiring views along Gold Camp Road, which is famous for its scenery.

enter North Cheyenne Canyon Park <5.0>. Continue through the first <5.6> and second <6.6> tunnels to a paved road <7.2>. Detour around closed tunnels Three, Four, and Five by turning left onto this paved road, following it down into the canyon to the boundary <10.3> of North Cheyenne Canyon Park. Just outside the boundary, turn right onto Evans Avenue (not the road to Seven Falls). Turn left onto Mesa Avenue <10.4>. Turn right onto Penrose Boulevard <10.6>. Continue straight on Penrose at a stop sign <11.0>. Turn right onto Old Stage Road <11.5> (not the road to the zoo) where Penrose meets Cheyenne Mountain Boulevard. Stay on the Old Stage Road to a T-intersection <18.5>; turn left to rejoin Gold Camp Road. Keep right <18.9> to bypass a private ranch. A large turnout <19.4>, marked by a metal sign as the beginning of the Saint Peters Dome Trail, offers good views to the east. The grade passes through exposed granite at Devil's Slide <20.5>. You may notice along here that the road crosses several trestles that were filled with earth to make the auto road. Go straight at an intersection <22.0> with a dirt road to the right marked by a sign identifying Victor (21 miles). Ignore a side road <24.2> on the right. Keep right <25.0> to stay on the main road. Continue through the sixth tunnel <31.8> to reach Cathedral Park <32.3>, perhaps the most scenic location along the road. The road bypasses the remains of a wooden trestle <38.2> and comes to a stop sign at the T-intersection <38.9>. A sign indicates a left turn for Victor and Cripple Creek and a right turn for Colorado Highway 67. Turn left and continue past another earth-filled trestle <39.3>. Go straight at an intersection <40.2> with a dirt road to the right. The pavement resumes <41.9> and leads into the mining towns of Victor and Cripple Creek (see site 42).

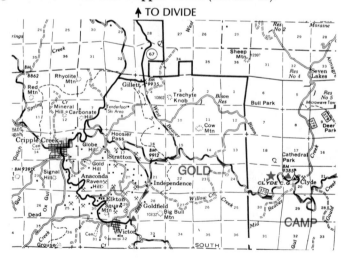

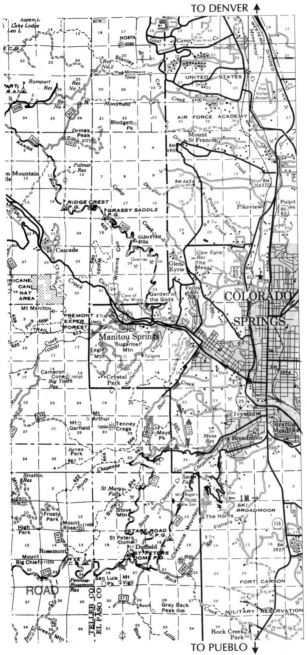

Courtesy of USDA Forest Service

# 47 UNITED STATES AIR FORCE ACADEMY

**TYPE:** Foothills Scenery/Historic
**ADMINISTRATION:** Military reservation
**QUALITY:** Scenic
**ACCESS:** Paved road
**FACILITIES:** Visitor Center
**TIME NEEDED:** Half day
**BEST VISIT:** Spring to fall
**BEST PHOTO:** Morning
**ELEVATION:** 7,170 feet (Chapel)
**REFERENCE:** Colorado Springs
**MAP:** State highway map
Pike National Forest visitor map
**USGS TOPO:** Pikeview 7.5' (1975)
Monument 7.5' (1975)
Palmer Lake 7.5' (1975)
**USGS COUNTY:** El Paso County Sheet 1 of 4 (1978)

The idea of an academy specially suited to the needs of the air service was first put forth by pioneer military aviators, including Brigadier General Billy Mitchell in the 1920s. It wasn't until 1949, however, that a panel of civilian and military educators was appointed by Secretary of Defense James Forrestal to recommend a general system of education for all of the armed forces. This board, chaired by Columbia University President Dwight D. Eisenhower and University of Colorado President Robert L. Stearns, reached the conclusion that the needs of the Air Force could not be met by expansion of the existing military academies. The board recommended that an Air Force academy be initiated without delay and that no less than 50 percent of officers commissioned into the services during peacetime be academy graduates.

In 1954, Congress appropriated funds to create the Air Force Academy. A commission was appointed by Secretary of the Air Force Harold E. Talbott to determine a suitable permanent site. The commissioners traveled 21,000 miles and considered 580 possible locations in 45 states before narrowing the potential selections to three sites. From these, the property near Colorado Springs was chosen by Talbott. One million dollars was contributed toward the purchase of the land by the State of Colorado. Temporary facilities were used at Lowry Air Force Base in Denver for the first entering Academy Class in 1955. In August 1958 cadets were able to occupy their permanent Academy home.

The first graduating class numbered 207 cadets, who were commissioned as second lieutenants in June of 1959. Today, over 4,000 cadets attend the academy, including, since 1976, women.

The course of study at the Academy is a four-year program resulting in a bachelor of science degree. The curriculum requires courses in basic sciences, engineering, social sciences, and humanities. The special needs of

The United States Air Force Academy Chapel is perhaps the most visited attraction in Colorado.

# 47 UNITED STATES AIR FORCE ACADEMY

the Air Force are served by coursework in human physiology, military history, astronautics, and other specialized classes. Physical education is also an extensive part of the cadet training program. The faculty of over 500 is composed largely of Air Force officers.

The grounds cover 18,000 acres of former ranch land. This region was once hunting grounds for many Indian tribes, including Ute, Arapahoe, Cheyenne, Kiowa, Comanche, Sioux, and Apache, though not all at the same time. It was not until the Colorado gold rush of 1859 that major settlement of the area began. A cabin dating from 1869 still stands on the Academy grounds.

The large size of the Academy accommodates the needs of various airmanship training programs, including airstrip placement. Private donations financed Falcon Stadium, a golf course, and recreational areas in the mountains west of the grounds. Modern architectural style using glass, aluminum, steel, and white marble is the theme of the Cadet Area buildings. The Cadet Chapel, with its 17 triangular spires, required five years of planning and four years of construction. The multi-denominational chapel is now a world-famous landmark. The Cadet Lunch Formation can be viewed at 12:05 PM on weekdays during the academic year from the chapel area.

**DIRECTIONS:** Visitors to the Academy should use the north entrance, accessible from exit 156B on Interstate 25, just north of Colorado Springs. After passing the guard station, continue straight to reach the Visitor Center (open daily from 9:00 AM to 5:00 PM, except Thanksgiving, Christmas, and New Year's days; the summer months may offer extended hours). From here, you are guided on a driving tour through the Academy by tour signs. You are allowed to stop in designated parking areas or at overlooks. In the main Cadet Area, only the Planetarium, Cadet Chapel, Cadet Social Center, and Field House are open to visitors. Services in the chapel are open to the public, and visitors are permitted to tour the chapel, which is usually open Monday through Saturday 9:00 AM to 5:00 PM and Sunday 1:00 PM to 5:00 PM. Free public shows are periodically given in the Planetarium.

A turnout for southbound traffic on Interstate 25 between the north and south Academy entrances offers an informative sign about Pikes Peak.

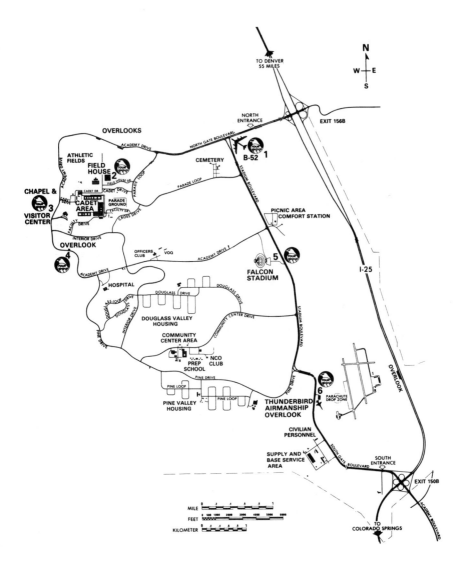

*Courtesy of United States Air Force Academy*

# 48 CALHAN PAINT MINES

TYPE: Plains Scenery/Geologic
ADMINISTRATION: Private land
QUALITY: Scenic
ACCESS: Good dirt road
FACILITIES: None
TIME NEEDED: One hour
BEST VISIT: Spring or fall
BEST PHOTO: Midday
ELEVATION: 6,725 feet (top of formations)
REFERENCE: Calhan
MAP: BLM Castle Rock 1:100,000
USGS TOPO: Calhan 7.5' (1970)
USGS COUNTY: El Paso County Sheet 2 of 4 (1976)

The Calhan Paint Mines are small gullies and dry washes cut through sedimentary layers of Colorado's eastern plains near the town of Calhan. The small canyons, less than 50 feet deep, are unexpectedly colorful for this normally drab region of the state. The strata are of the Dawson formation, deposited in Tertiary times. The pillars and steep walls of Dawson clay are protected by a cap layer of white cross-bedded sandstone. These clays, primarily stained by iron oxides, are brightly colored in hues of red, purple, orange, yellow, brown, and gray. Embedded gypsum crystals help lighten certain layers.

The Paint Mines get their name from the belief that local Plains Indians visited here to get "paint" from the richly pigmented clays. Arrow heads and other artifacts have been found in the vicinity, but there is no direct proof that pigments have been mined.

Although the Paint Mines are on private property, the public is allowed to visit, provided that no vehicles are used, visitors do not wander elsewhere on the property, and no trash or litter is left behind. If you should visit the Paint Mines and find the area closed, enjoy the scenery from the public road only. Please respect the generosity of the landowner.

DIRECTIONS: From Colorado Springs, proceed east on US 24 to the town of Calhan. A green sign <0.0> showing the town name and elevation (6,507 feet) is located at the western boundary of Calhan. Continue through the town to an intersection <0.9> with a paved road to the right just at the eastern edge of town before mile-marker 340. Turn right onto this road, marked by a street sign as the Calhan Highway. Continue past the county fairgrounds on the right. Turn left onto a good dirt road marked by a street sign as Paint Mine Road at its intersection <1.5> just past the fairgrounds. The road makes a sharp curve <2.5> to the right and then comes to a fork <3.4>. Take the left fork and pull over to the left side of the road at a cattle guard <3.6>. Walk through the cattle guard and down into the Paint Mines area.

The miniature canyon system of the Calhan Paint Mines is intricate and colorful.

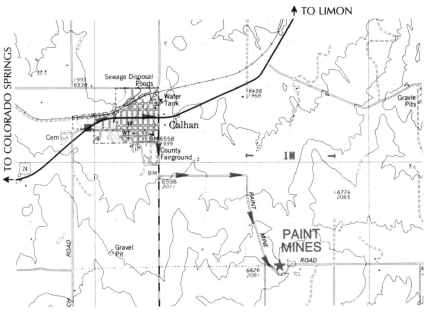

*Courtesy of USGS*

# 49 CANON CITY PARKS

**TYPE:** Mountain Scenery/Geologic/Historic
**ADMINISTRATION:** Public land—Canon City Parks
**QUALITY:** Scenic
**ACCESS:** Good dirt road
**FACILITIES:** Picnic areas at Temple and Red Canyon Parks
**TIME NEEDED:** One day
**BEST VISIT:** Spring to fall
**BEST PHOTO:** All day
**ELEVATION:** 5,856 feet (Skyline Drive)
**REFERENCE:** Canon City
**MAP:** BLM Canon City 1:100,000
BLM Pikes Peak 1:100,000
**USGS TOPO:** Canon City 7.5' (1976)
Royal Gorge 15' (1959)
Cover Mountain 15' (1942)
Cooper Mountain 7.5' (1954)
**USGS COUNTY:** Fremont County Sheet 2 of 3 (1980)
Fremont County Sheet 3 of 3 (1980)

In addition to Royal Gorge (see site 50), Canon City (pronounced Canyon City) maintains four other points of interest for the sightseer. These scenic locations are Skyline Drive, Tunnel Drive, Red Canyon Park, and Temple Canyon Park. Skyline Drive and Tunnel Drive are near the city, while Red Canyon Park and Temple Canyon Park require short drives into the surrounding countryside.

Skyline Drive is a one-lane road built on the top of a narrow hogback that borders the west side of the city. John C. Fremont climbed this ridge to plant an American flag during his 1846 Colorado expedition. The scenic road was completed in 1906 by inmates of the nearby state penitentiary. The masonry arch at the drive's entrance contains a sample stone from each of the nation's states. This sometimes exciting road has several turnouts with good views of the surrounding area. Nearby, fossil fish skeletons dating back 500 million years have been found. Skyline Drive is open from early morning to sunset, as weather permits, and is not recommended for large or heavy vehicles.

Tunnel Drive is a short road that follows a gentle grade from the city into the eastern portal of the Grand Canyon of the Arkansas River (Royal Gorge). Visitors can drive through a pair of closely spaced tunnels that were originally blasted by a private ditch company for water diversion to a new housing development east of the city. The company went bankrupt, and the city, using convict labor, turned the project into a scenic drive. The road ends a few miles inside the canyon, where it meets the tracks of the Denver and Rio Grande Western Railroad.

Red Canyon Park is a 500-acre city park north of town containing interesting formations of a conglomerate sedimentary layer made of small stone

Grape Creek cuts a scenic canyon through Temple Canyon Park.

# 49 CANON CITY PARKS

Built atop a hogback west of Canon City, single-lane Skyline Drive is a scenic and entertaining driving experience.

Red Canyon Park exhibits numerous deep red rock formations that are weathered into interesting pillars and shapes.

This pair of closely spaced tunnels give Tunnel Drive its name.

# 49  CANON CITY PARKS

chunks cemented together by large quantities of deep red sandstone. The park offers picnic areas, hiking, and sightseeing opportunities. To reach the park, you will drive through an area known as Garden Park, where discoveries of dinosaur fossils in 1876 made worldwide history. Paleontologists Edward Cope and Charles Marsh unearthed more than five species of giant reptiles, including the Stegosaurus, Allosaurus, Ceratosaurus, Camptosaurus, and Brontosaurus.

Located southwest of town, 640-acre Temple Canyon Park offers picnic areas and the impressive scenery of Grape Creek Canyon, which is cut through colorful Precambrian granite. The park is named for a natural amphitheater, or temple, in a side canyon to the north of Grape Creek. Legend holds that a duel was fought in the temple between chiefs of the Ute and Blackfoot tribes over the fate of the Indian maiden Lachita. Indian arrowheads and pictographs have been found within the park.

**DIRECTIONS:** To reach Skyline Drive, proceed west on US 50 from Canon City. From the state penitentiary <0.0> at the west end of town, continue west to a junction <3.0> with a paved road to the right marked by a sign as Skyline Drive. Turn here and start climbing the hogback. The paved one-lane road follows the ridge of the hogback and descends back into Canon City via switchbacks. The road deposits you onto 5th Street, where a right turn will allow you to return to US 50.

To reach Tunnel Drive, proceed west on US 50 from Canon City. Continue around the curve just past the state penitentiary <0.0> at the west end of town. Immediately after this curve, turn left onto a paved road <0.5> marked by a sign identifying this as the turn for Tunnel Drive. Cross a small bridge and continue straight on this paved road. Just past a building on the right, there is a dirt road <1.1> to the right that climbs a hill. Turn right and follow this road up the hill to where it joins a nearly level grade. The road passes through a pair of tunnels as it enters the Grand Canyon of the Arkansas. The road ends after a few miles, and you must return by the same route.

To reach Temple Canyon Park, proceed west on US 50 from Canon City. Continue past the state penitentiary <0.0> at the western end of town, past the road <9.2> to Royal Gorge (see site 50), and past the junction <10.3> with Colorado Highway 9. Follow US 50 downhill to an intersection with a paved road on tl e left just after crossing a bridge over the Arkansas River in Parkdale. Turn left at this junction <12.2> and follow paved Fremont County 3 past a dirt road <14.6> on the right to the intersection <15.8> of another dirt road on the right. Turn right, leaving the pavement, and follow this dirt road to the entrance <18.8> of Temple Canyon Park (marked by a sign). This road may become muddy when wet. The road continues through the park and eventually returns to Canon City; however, it becomes rougher beyond the park.

# 49  CANON CITY PARKS

To reach Red Canyon Park, enter the east end of Canon City by traveling westbound on US 50. Just after passing the Holy Cross Abbey <0.0>, take the first right at a stop light onto Raynolds Avenue. Before you finish this turn, make a left turn onto the service road (Fremont Drive) that parallels and nearly touches US 50 on its north side. Continue for half a block and turn right onto Fields Avenue <0.2>. Continue north on Fields and go straight at each of the stop signs. Go straight where a road merges from the left; you are now on Fremont County 9, whose pavement comes and goes in segments. A historical marker <6.6> identifies Garden Park, site of several dinosaur skeleton discoveries. Continue on the main road to the junction with a dirt road <10.1> to the left marked by a small red sign (on the right) as the turn for Red Canyon Park. Turn left and follow this road to the park boundary <10.5>. The main dirt road through the park winds among the formations but does not loop back to the main entrance. The road inside the park may be muddy when wet. You should return by retracing your route.

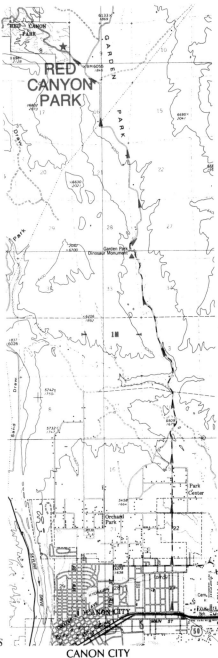

Courtesy of USGS

CANON CITY

# 49 CANON CITY PARKS

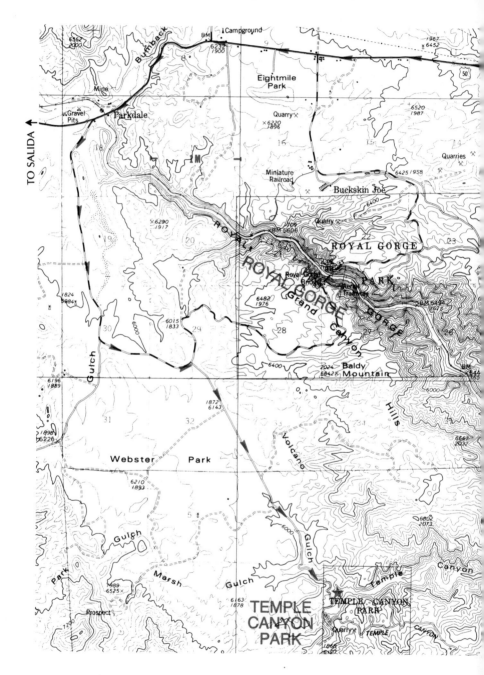

# CANON CITY PARKS

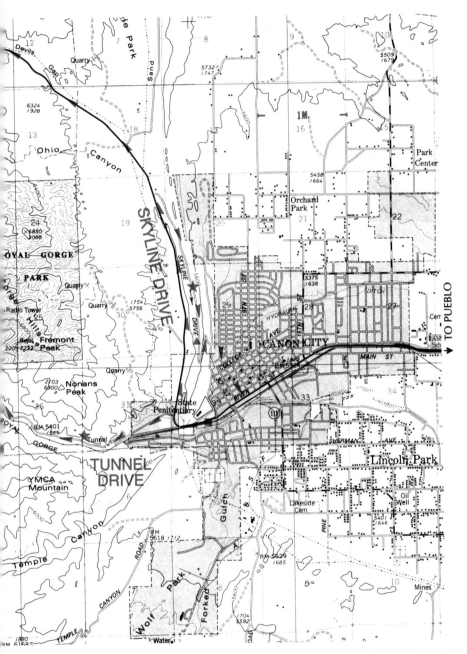

*Courtesy of USGS*

# 50 ROYAL GORGE

**TYPE:** Mountain Scenery/Geologic/Historic
**ADMINISTRATION:** Public land—Canon City Park
**QUALITY:** Very scenic
**ACCESS:** Paved road
**FACILITIES:** Commercial attractions/Picnic areas
**TIME NEEDED:** Half day
**BEST VISIT:** All year
**BEST PHOTO:** Midday
**ELEVATION:** 6,400 feet (rim)
**REFERENCE:** Canon City
**MAP:** State highway map
BLM Canon City 1:100,000
**USGS TOPO:** Royal Gorge 15' (1959)
**USGS COUNTY:** Fremont County Sheet 2 of 3 (1980)

Royal Gorge, or Grand Canyon of the Arkansas River, is one of the deepest canyons in Colorado. It is cut over 1,250 feet through Precambrian granite. The course of the Arkansas River was already well established when the uplift of this granite began. The river slowly cut this canyon as the rock mass between Parkdale and Canon City rose above the level of the flowing water. It is estimated that this uplift happened at the rate of one foot every 2,500 years. The resulting seven-mile-long gorge has nearly vertical walls separated approximately 50 feet at the bottom and a few hundred feet at the rim.

This area was known to Colorado's mountain tribe, the Utes, and the many plains tribes, including Blackfoot, Comanche, Kiowa, Sioux, and Cheyenne, who occasionally followed the Arkansas Valley to the gorge. Early Spanish explorers and mountain men probably also enjoyed the dramatic scenery of the gorge. The first recorded visit to Royal Gorge was made by Lieutenant Zebulon Montgomery Pike in the winter of 1806. Having followed the Arkansas River to the eastern portal of the canyon, Pike set up base camp and dispatched a scouting party into the gorge. They returned and reported that it was impossible to negotiate the canyon. The expedition set off cross-country to avoid this obstacle and eventually made its way to the headwaters of the Arkansas River. They mistakenly believed it to be the Red River, and it was not until a month later when they followed the river back to the western portal of Royal Gorge that they realized their mistake. Later, Lieutenant John C. Fremont explored this region seeking a route for a transcontinental railroad.

A war of sorts was fought inside the canyon between the Atchison, Topeka, and Santa Fe Railroad and the Denver and Rio Grande Railroad. With the discovery of silver in Leadville, there was considerable incentive to locate a rail line to the headwaters of the Arkansas River. Both of these railroads took an interest in this possibility, but one problem stood in the way: there was barely enough room through the Royal Gorge for a single set of tracks, much less two. So, a brisk competition began between the Rio Grande and the

Royal Gorge Bridge, the highest suspension span in the world, crosses the Grand Canyon of the Arkansas 1,053 feet above the river.

# 50 ROYAL GORGE

Santa Fe. Work crews representing each railroad converged on the eastern portal of the gorge on the same day in April 1879. The Santa Fe crew arrived first by a few minutes and forced the Rio Grande team to retreat. Undaunted, the displaced crew sneaked past the Santa Fe camp, and both groups had leveled roadbed in the canyon by nightfall. Under the cover of darkness, saboteurs from each camp unknowingly crept past each other and almost simultaneously dynamited each other's progress. Forts built of rock and railroad ties began to appear, and gunfire was exchanged. Simultaneously, a court battle was waged for legal control of this right-of-way. After nearly eight months of conflict, an agreement was reached between the opposing parties, giving the Denver and Rio Grande control over the route.

Most visitors enjoyed the gorge scenery from the tracks of the Rio Grande until completion of the world's highest suspension bridge in 1929. This project was accomplished in less than a year at a cost of $350,000, using materials made by Colorado Fuel and Iron Corporation in Pueblo. The 18-foot-wide bridge is 1,260 feet long, with 880 feet of the main span between two 150-foot towers. The 1,053-foot-high roadbed is made of 1,292 wooden planks. The bridge can support over 2 million pounds. The same construction crew then began work on the world's steepest incline railway, completed in 1931. Up to 30 passengers can descend to the bottom of the gorge in the specially designed cars. In 1969, an aerial tramway was strung across the chasm to ferry sightseers from rim to rim, 1,200 feet above the river.

Today, Royal Gorge is encompassed by a 5,120-acre park owned by Canon City. The park has picnic areas, hiking trails, and commercial attractions. The Royal Gorge bridge, incline railway, and tramway are also owned by the city and are operated by the Royal Gorge Bridge Company. These three adventures can be enjoyed for a nominal fee.

**DIRECTIONS:** From Canon City, proceed west on US 50 and pass the state penitentiary <0.0> at the west end of town. Continue past a side road <0.5> on the left that goes to Tunnel Drive (see site 49) and past a side road <3.0> on the right for Skyline Drive (see site 49). The entrance road to Royal Gorge off US 50 is well marked. Turn left (south) at this intersection <9.2> and follow paved Fremont County 3A to the park boundary <11.9>, marked by a sign. Several picnic areas are on both sides of the road, and one on the left <12.8> is scenically located on the rim of the canyon. Continue on the paved road to visit the bridge, incline railway, and tramway.

If you are west of Royal Gorge, proceed eastbound on US 50. Continue past the junction <0.0> with Colorado Highway 9 to the well-marked entrance road to Royal Gorge. Turn right (south) at this intersection <1.2> and follow the paved road to the park boundary <3.9>. Continuing a short distance farther will bring you to the bridge, incline railway, and tramway.

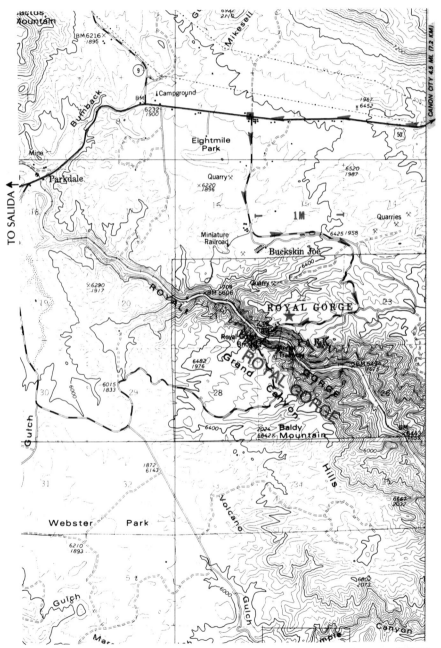

*Courtesy of USGS*

# SUMMARY

| DISTRICT | SITE NUMBER AND NAME | SCENERY | ADMIN. | QUALITY | ACCESS | HOURS | VISIT | PHOTO |
|---|---|---|---|---|---|---|---|---|
| North-west | 1 Irish Canyon | TGH | B | V | G | 1 | SF | M |
| | 2 Dinosaur National Monument | TGO | M | * | P | 16 | SF | MA |
| | 3 Cañon Pintado | THO | B | S | P | .5 | SF | M |
| Steamboat Springs | 4 Trappers Lake | T | F | V | G | 1 | EJLF | A |
| | 5 Fish Creek Falls | M | FX | V | G | .5 | J | A |
| | 6 Rabbit Ears Peak | MG | F | S | P | .5 | EJLF | MD |
| | 7 Finger Rock | G | BX | S | P | .2 | SEJLF | AL |
| | 8 Gore Canyon | MH | BX | V | G | .5 | SEJLF | A |
| Front Range | 9 Natural Fort | PGH | * | S | P | .5 | SEJLFW | EMDAL |
| | 10 Pawnee Buttes | PGO | GX | S | G | .5 | SF | AL |
| | 11 Nokhu Crags | M | * | V | P | .5 | SEJLF | AL |
| | 12 Devils Backbone | FG | X | S | P | .2 | SF | AL |
| | 13 Rocky Mountain National Park | M | P | E | P | 8 | EJLF | EMDAL |
| | 14 Indian Peaks | M | F | V | P | 1 | EJLF | M |
| | 15 Boulder Falls | M | * | S | P | .5 | J | DA |
| | 16 Royal Arch | FG | * | S | PH | 4 | SEJLF | M |
| | 17 Moffat Road | MH | FX | V | R | 4 | JL | EMDAL |
| | 18 Central City | MH | X | S | P | 4 | SEJLF | MD |
| | 19 Georgetown | MH | X | S | P | 4 | SEJLF | D |
| | 20 Mount Evans Highway | M | F | V | P | 4 | JL | EMDAL |

**SCENERY**
M: Mountains
F: Foothills
P: Plains
T: Plateau
G: Geologic
H: Historic
O: Other

**ADMINISTRATION**
P: Natl Park
M: Natl Monument
R: Natl Rec Area
F: Natl Forest
G: Natl Grassland
B: BLM
U: US Military
*: Public Land
X: Private Land

**QUALITY**
*: Superbly Scenic
E: Extremely Scenic
V: Very Scenic
S: Scenic

**ACCESS**
P: Paved Road
G: Good Dirt Road
D: Dirt Road
R: Rough Dirt Road
E: Easy 4WD
M: Moderate 4WD
4: Difficult 4WD
H: Hike

# SUMMARY

| DISTRICT | SITE NUMBER AND NAME | SCENERY | ADMIN. | QUALITY | ACCESS | HOURS | VISIT | PHOTO |
|---|---|---|---|---|---|---|---|---|
| Glenwood Springs | 21 Rifle Falls | TG | * | S | P | 4 | SEJLF | D |
| | 22 Glenwood Canyon | TG | F | V | P | 1 | SEJLF | M |
| | 23 Hanging Lake | TG | F | E | PH | 4 | SEJLF | D |
| | 24 Deep Creek Overlook | TG | F | S | G | .5 | EJLF | MD |
| | 25 Mount Sopris | M | F | S | P | .2 | SEJLF | A |
| | 26 Marble | MGH | **X | E | P | 8 | EJLF | MD |
| | 27 Crystal | MH | FX | V | EH | 1 | EJLF | A |
| | 28 Maroon Bells | MG | F | E | P | 1 | EJLF | M |
| | 29 Ashcroft | MH | F | S | P | 1 | EJLF | M |
| | 30 Grottos | MG | F | S | P | 1 | EJLF | D |
| | 31 Independence Pass | M | F | V | P | .5 | EJLF | A |
| Leadville | 32 Mount of the Holy Cross | MH | F | E | RH | 4 | J | M |
| | 33 Red Cone | MH | FX | S | M | 4 | JL | DA |
| | 34 Mount Guyot | MH | F | S | G | .5 | JL | M |
| | 35 Bristlecone Pine Scenic Area | MO | F | S | D | .5 | JL | D |
| | 36 Mosquito Pass | MH | FX | V | M | 1 | JL | MD |
| | 37 Chalk Cliffs | MG | FX | S | P | .5 | SEJLF | MD |
| | 38 Saint Elmo | MH | X | S | G | 1 | EJLF | MDA |
| | 39 Monarch Pass | M | F | S | P | .5 | EJLF | A |
| Colorado Springs | 40 Lost Creek Scenic Area | MG | F | S | GH | 8 | EJLF | MD |
| | 41 Florissant Fossil Beds | MO | M | S | G | 4 | SEJLF | M |
| | 42 Cripple Creek | MH | X | S | P | 4 | SEJLF | D |
| | 43 Pikes Peak | MH | F | S | G | 4 | JL | M |
| | 44 Cave of the Winds | G | X | S | P | 2 | SEJLFW | D |
| | 45 Garden of the Gods | FG | * | E | P | 4 | SEJLF | EMDAL |
| | 46 Gold Camp Road | MH | FX | V | G | 4 | EJLF | MD |
| | 47 United States Air Force Academy | FH | U | S | P | 4 | SEJLF | M |
| | 48 Calhan Paint Mines | PG | X | S | G | 1 | SF | M |
| | 49 Canon City Parks | MGH | * | S | G | 8 | SEJLF | EMDAL |
| | 50 Royal Gorge | MGH | *X | V | P | 4 | SEJLFW | D |

**VISIT**
S: Spring     L: Late Summer
E: Early Summer     F: Fall
J: July     W: Winter

**PHOTO**
E: Early Morning     A: Afternoon
M: Morning     L: Late Afternoon
D: Midday

# MAP DATA

Page: Map Name

30, 31: USGS State of Colorado 1:500,000
35: BLM NW-1 Surface Management Quad
41: NPS Dinosaur National Monument
45: BLM NW-13 Surface Management Quad
46, 47: USGS State of Colorado 1:500,000
50, 51: White River National Forest Visitor Map
55 Top: USGS Routt County Sheet 4 of 5
55 Bottom, 59: Routt National Forest Visitor Map
63: USGS Routt County Sheet 5 of 5
67: Routt National Forest Visitor Map
68, 69: USGS State of Colorado 1:500,000
73: USGS Weld County Sheet 1 of 7
77: Pawnee National Grassland Visitor Map
80, 81, 83, 87: Roosevelt National Forest Visitor Map
91: Arapaho National Forest Visitor Map
93: Roosevelt National Forest Visitor Map
97: USGS Boulder County
100, 101, 103, 105, 109: Arapaho National Forest Visitor Map
110, 111: USGS State of Colorado 1:500,000
115, 117, 121 top: White River National Forest Visitor Map
121 bottom: USGS Garfield County Sheet 5 of 5
124, 125, 127, 133, 137, 141, 145: White River National Forest Visitor Map
147: USGS Pitkin County Sheet 2 of 2
150, 151: White River National Forest Visitor Map
152, 153: USGS State of Colorado 1:500,000
157: White River National Forest Visitor Map
161, 163, 165: Pike National Forest Visitor Map
168, 169, 171, 174, 175: San Isabel National Forest Visitor Map
177, 178, 179: USGS State of Colorado 1:500,000
182, 183: Pike National Forest Visitor Map
187: NPS Florissant Fossil Beds National Monument
191, 193: Pike National Forest Visitor Map
195, 199: USGS El Paso County Sheet 1 of 4
202, 203: Pike National Forest Visitor Map
207: United States Air Force Academy
209: USGS El Paso County Sheet 2 of 4
215: USGS Fremont County Sheet 3 of 3
216: USGS Fremont County Sheet 2 of 3
217: USGS Fremont County Sheet 3 of 3
221: USGS Fremont County Sheet 2 of 3

# MAP SOURCES

National Forest and National Grassland Visitor Maps:
Visitor Map Sales
USDA Forest Service
P.O. Box 25127
Lakewood, Colorado 80225

USGS Maps:
USGS Map Sales
Building 810
Denver Federal Center
Denver, Colorado 80225

BLM Maps:
Bureau of Land Management
Colorado State Office
2850 Youngfield Street
Denver, Colorado 80215

NPS Maps:
National Park Service
United States Department of the Interior
12795 W. Alameda Parkway
P.O. Box 25287
Denver, Colorado 80225

State Highway Map:
State Department of Highways
4201 East Arkansas Avenue
Denver, Colorado 80222

# PHOTOGRAPHIC CREDITS

Page: Subject and from where taken, source, time of day, month, year.

Front cover: Maroon Bells, Barbara Johnson, midday, 1980.

6: Rocky Mountain National Park, National Park Service.

13 top: Satellite photo of Colorado, USGS Conterminous United States NASA ERTS-1, Satellite Image Mosaic, Band 7-Summer, 1974.

13 bottom: Geologic zones of Colorado, Colorado Geological Survey Bulletin 32, *Prairie, Peak, and Plateau*, 1972.

33 top: Irish Canyon from just inside southern end of Irish Canyon, Lee Gregory, morning, September, 1982.

33 bottom: Irish Canyon petroglyphs from east side of boulder, Lee Gregory, morning, July, 1982.

37 top: Echo Park from Harpers Corner overlook, Lee Gregory, September, 1979.

37 bottom: Dinosaur bones inside Dinosaur Quarry Visitor Center, Lee Gregory, midday, August, 1977.

38: Whirlpool Canyon from Harpers Corner overlook, Colorado Office of Tourism.

39: Gates of Lodore from the end of the nature trail at Lodore Campground, Lee Gregory, morning, July, 1989.

43: Cañon Pintado petroglyphs, Lee Gregory, morning, September, 1982.

49: Trappers Lake from its north shore, Bureau of Land Management.

53: Fish Creek Falls from the trail, Lee Gregory, afternoon, June, 1989.

57: Rabbit Ears Peak from about a mile north of the old pass marker, Lee Gregory, morning, October, 1980.

61: Finger Rock as seen from the north along the highway, Lee Gregory, late afternoon, June, 1989.

65: West end of Gore Canyon from Inspiration Point, Lee Gregory, afternoon, August, 1980.

71 top: West side of Natural Fort at the eastern rest area, Lee Gregory, afternoon, April, 1980.

71 bottom: Northeast corner of Natural Fort at the eastern rest area, Lee Gregory, morning, September, 1982.

75 top: Pawnee Buttes from a ridge to the southwest, Lee Gregory, midday, September, 1982.

75 bottom: East Pawnee Butte from between the buttes, Lee Gregory, afternoon, October, 1980.

79: Nokhu Crags from the scenic turnout east of Cameron Pass, Lee Gregory, morning, August, 1980.

83: Northern end of Devils Backbone from its west side, Lee Gregory, afternoon, September, 1979.

# PHOTOGRAPHIC CREDITS

85 top: Bear Lake from its northwest shore, Lee Gregory, afternoon, October, 1979.

85 bottom: Hiking trail about a quarter mile from Chasm Lake, Lee Gregory, morning, July, 1978.

89: Indian Peaks from the informative sign, Lee Gregory, morning, September, 1982.

93: Boulder Falls from the trail, Colorado Office of Tourism.

95: Royal Arch from its southern side, Lee Gregory, late morning, April, 1982.

99: Devil's Slide Trestle from road, Lee Gregory, afternoon, July, 1978.

103: Central City from a hill to the southeast, Colorado Office of Tourism.

105: Georgetown from a low switchback on the Guanella Pass road, Lee Gregory, midday, October, 1980.

107 top: Summit Lake from its northeast shore, Lee Gregory, morning, August, 1977.

107 bottom: Echo Lake from a ridge to the northeast, Colorado Office of Tourism.

113 top: Rifle Falls from the southeast, Lee Gregory, afternoon, August, 1979.

113 bottom: Inside Rifle Falls Cave, Lee Gregory, afternoon, August, 1979.

117: Looking east through Glenwood Canyon from Hanging Lake parking area, Lee Gregory, afternoon, July, 1989.

119: Spouting Rock from the northwest, Lee Gregory, afternoon, July, 1989.

120: Hanging Lake from its southern rim, Lee Gregory, afternoon, July, 1989.

123: Deep Creek from the eastern Deep Creek overlook, Lee Gregory, morning, September, 1982.

127: Mount Sopris from a turnout south of Carbondale, Steve Reames, afternoon, August, 1980.

129 top: Yule marble quarry from the top of a nearby marble pile, Lee Gregory, midday, August, 1978.

129 bottom: Mill from the bridge across the Crystal River, Lee Gregory, morning, August, 1978.

130: Interior of Yule marble quarry, Lee Gregory, midday, August, 1981.

131: Yule Creek just east of the quarry, Lee Gregory, midday, September, 1978.

133: Marble Mill site, Colorado Office of Tourism.

135: Power station just west of Crystal from the north bank of the Crystal River, Colorado Office of Tourism.

139: Maroon Bells from Maroon Lake, Colorado Office of Tourism.

141: Maroon Bells from Maroon Lake, Bureau of Land Management.

# PHOTOGRAPHIC CREDITS

143: Ashcroft from the southwest, Colorado Office of Tourism.

147: Interior of the Grottos, Lee Gregory, midday, August, 1979.

149: View looking east from Independence Pass overlook, Lee Gregory, afternoon, September, 1982.

155: Mount of the Holy Cross from the northwestern side of Notch Mountain, Lee Gregory, morning, July, 1982.

159: Handcart Peak from the basin to the southeast, Lee Gregory, midday, August, 1982.

160: Red Cone from the base of a rock glacier on the southwestern side of Red Cone, Lee Gregory, midday, August, 1982.

163: Mount Guyot from about 2 miles east of Georgia Pass, Lee Gregory, morning, August, 1989.

165: Looking northeast through the bristlecones on Windy Ridge, Lee Gregory, afternoon, September, 1980.

167 top: North London Mine boarding house from the road, Lee Gregory, midday September, 1989.

167 bottom: Sign at Mosquito Pass, Lee Gregory, midday, September, 1980.

171: Chalk Cliffs from the road, Lee Gregory, late morning, July, 1981.

173 top: Looking northeast across Saint Elmo's main street, Colorado Office of Tourism.

173 bottom: Buildings at eastern end of Saint Elmo, Lee Gregory, midday, July, 1981.

177: Looking northeast from Monarch Pass, Lee Gregory, afternoon, June, 1978.

181 top: Scenery along Goose Creek about a mile from the trailhead, Lee Gregory, midday, September, 1982.

181 bottom: Rock formation between the trail and Goose Creek about 2.5 miles from the trailhead, Lee Gregory, midday, July, 1979.

185: The Trio from the southeast, Lee Gregory, morning, July, 1982.

186: Fossil wasp, Walter Saenger, Florissant Fossil Beds National Monument.

189 top: Cripple Creek from south of town along the highway, Lee Gregory, morning, September, 1982.

189 bottom: Mining ruins on Battle Mountain from Goldfield, Lee Gregory, morning, September, 1982.

193: Pikes Peak from northeast of the Gateway Rocks in Garden of the Gods, Pikes Peak Country Attractions Association.

195: Canopy Hall in Cave of the Winds, Ken Scott, *The Sun Newspaper*, Colorado Springs (courtesy of Grant Carey, Cave of the Winds), August, 1972.

# PHOTOGRAPHIC CREDITS

197: Balanced Rock from the south, Lee Gregory, late morning, April, 1978.
199: Gateway Rocks from the southeast, Lee Gregory, late morning, April, 1978.
201: Cathedral Park from the road, Lee Gregory, morning, September, 1989.
205: USAFA Chapel, Denver Convention and Visitors Bureau.
209: Inside a western side canyon in Calhan Paint Mines, Lee Gregory, late morning, August, 1978.
211: Grape Creek Canyon from its south rim near the middle of the park, Lee Gregory, early afternoon, July, 1979.
212 top: Skyline Drive from the road, Lee Gregory, midday, June, 1978.
212 bottom: Looking northeast across Red Canyon Park, Lee Gregory, midday, September, 1982.
213: Pair of tunnels on Tunnel Drive, Lee Gregory, midday, June, 1982.
219: Royal Gorge and Bridge from the tram, Lee Gregory, afternoon, May, 1978.

Back Cover (from left to right):
Bighorn lamb near Fall River entrance, Rocky Mountain National Park, Bob Schram, midday, September, 1979.
James Peak from Rollins Pass, Nancy White, morning, July, 1978.
East side of Independence Pass from Twin Lakes, Bob Schram, afternoon, October, 1988.
Columbines north of Steamboat Springs, Nancy White, afternoon, September, 1980.

# SUGGESTED READING

Agnew, Jeremy. *Exploring the Colorado High Country*. Colorado Springs: Wildwood Press, 1977.

Athearn, Robert G. *The Denver and Rio Grande Western Railroad*. Lincoln: University of Nebraska Press, 1962.

Bancroft, Caroline. *Unique Ghost Towns and Mountain Spots*. Boulder: Johnson Publishing, 1961.

Bollinger, Edward T. *Rails That Climb: A Narrative History of the Moffat Road*. Golden, Colo.: Colorado Railroad Museum, 1979.

Borneman, Walter R., and Lampert, Lyndon J. *A Climbing Guide to Colorado's Fourteeners*. Boulder: Pruett Publishing, 1978.

Brown, Robert L. *Colorado Ghost Towns: Past and Present*. Caldwell, Id.: Caxton Printers, 1972.

———. *Ghost Towns of the Colorado Rockies*. Caldwell, Id.: Caxton Printers, 1968.

———. *Holy Cross: The Mountain and the City*. Caldwell, Id.: Caxton Printers, 1970.

———. *Jeep Trails to Colorado Ghost Towns*. Caldwell, Id.: Caxton Printers, 1963.

Bueler, Gladys R. *Colorado's Colorful Characters*. Boulder: Pruett Publishing, 1981.

Chapman, Joe, and Chapman, Dinah Jo. *The Royal Gorge*. Canon City, Colo.: Royal Gorge Company, 1965.

Chronic, Halka. *Roadside Geology of Colorado*. Missoula: Mountain Press Publishing, 1980. (excellent traveling guide)

Chronic, John, and Chronic, Halka. *Prairie, Peak and Plateau: A Guide to the Geology of Colorado* (Colorado Geological Survey Bulletin 32). Denver: Colorado Geological Survey, 1972.

Davidson, James Dale. *An Eccentric Guide to the United States*. New York: Berkley Publishing, 1977.

Eberhart, Perry. *Guide to the Colorado Ghost Towns and Mining Camps*. Chicago: Swallow Press, 1969. (excellent traveling guide)

Feitz, Leland. *Cripple Creek: A Quick History of the World's Greatest Gold Camp*. Colorado Springs: Little London Press, 1967.

Grout, William. *Colorado Adventures: Forty Trips in the Rockies*. Denver: Golden Bell Press, 1973.

Hansen, Harry (ed.). *Colorado: A Guide to the Highest State*. New York: Hastings House, 1970. (excellent traveling guide)

Helmers, Dow. *Historic Alpine Tunnel*. Colorado Springs: Century One Press, 1971.

Lavender, David. *David Lavender's Colorado*. Garden City, N.Y.: Doubleday, 1976.

Nesbit, Paul W. *Garden of God's*. Boulder: N. L. Nesbit, 1973.

Parris, Lloyd E. *Caves of Colorado*. Boulder: Pruett Publishing, 1973.

Pearl, Richard M. *America's Mountain: Pikes Peak and the Pikes Peak Region*. Denver: Sage Books, 1964.

# SUGGESTED READING

_____. *Colorado Gem Trails and Mineral Guide*. Chicago: Swallow Press, 1968.

_____. *Exploring Rocks, Minerals, Fossils in Colorado*. Chicago: Swallow Press, 1969.

_____. *Landforms of Colorado*. Colorado Springs: Earth Science Publishing, 1975.

Powell, John Wesley. *The Exploration of the Colorado River and Its Canyons*. New York: Dover Publications, 1961 (reprint).

Redford, Robert. *The Outlaw Trail*. New York: Grosset and Dunlap, 1978.

Roberts, Jack. *The Amazing Adventures of Lord Gore: A True Saga from the Old West*. Denver: Sundance Publications, 1977.

Sprague, Marshall. *The Great Gates: The Story of the Rocky Mountain Passes*. Lincoln: University of Nebraska Press, 1964.

Sykes, Jr., George K., and Sumner, David. *Guide to Natural Wonders of the West*. Harrisburg, Penn.: Stackpole Books, 1978.

Vandenbusche, Duane, and Myers, Rex. *Marble, Colorado: City of Stone*. Denver: Golden Bell Press, 1970.

# INFORMATION SOURCES

USDA Forest Service
Rocky Mountain Region
11177 West 8th Avenue
P.O. Box 25127
Lakewood, Colorado 80225

Bureau of Land Management
Colorado State Office
2850 Youngfield Street
Denver, Colorado 80215

National Park Service
United States Department of the Interior
12795 W. Alameda Parkway
P.O. Box 25287
Denver, Colorado 80225

National Cartographic Information Center
United States Geological Survey
Box 25046, Stop 504
Denver Federal Center
Denver, Colorado 80225

Colorado Tourism Board
1625 Broadway, Suite 1700
Denver, Colorado 80202

Colorado Geological Survey
Department of Natural Resources
715 State Centennial Building
1313 Sherman Street
Denver, Colorado 80203

State of Colorado
Division of Parks and Outdoor Recreation
Room 618
1313 Sherman Street
Denver, Colorado 80203

United States Air Force Academy
Colorado Springs, Colorado 80840

# INDEX

# INDEX

# INDEX

# INDEX

# INDEX

# INDEX

# INDEX

# STATE MAP

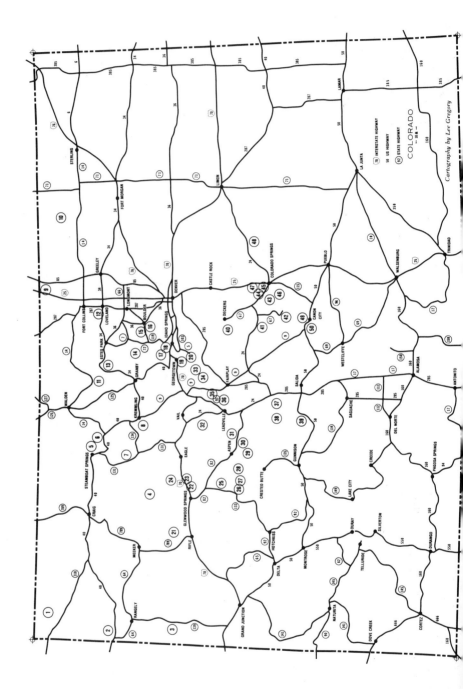

Cartography by Lee Gregory

COLORADO
— 108 —

78  INTERSTATE HIGHWAY
50  US HIGHWAY
82  STATE HIGHWAY